D1067905

FROM MUSIC BOXES TO STREET ORGANS

MR. R. DE WAARD

From music boxes to street organs

Translated from the Dutch by Wade Jenkins

SEO Library Center
State Library of Ohio
40780 Marietta Road, Caldwell, OH 43724

English edition published by

The Vestal Press   Vestal, New York 13850   u.s.a.

Photographs in this book by F. Posthumus, Den Haag;
M. van Boxtel, Nijmegen; Louis van Paridon, Amsterdam;
and others.

English edition Copyright © 1967 by The Vestal Press

Library of Congress Card Catalog Number

67-27808

The special appeal

of this instrument

is that its music

is equally tranquilizing,

no matter what the time of

day may be: moments of relaxation

or moments of seriousness.

HENDRIK ANDRIESSEN ABOUT THE PIEREMENT

(this book originally published in Dutch by De Toorts,
Haarlem, the Netherlands)

Contents

PREFACE TO THE ENGLISH EDITION

Since 1961 when the Vestal Press was founded, it has brought to the music-loving public several books and many paper-back brochures dealing with the history and the technicalities of automatic musical instruments of many varieties. Many of its customers have been most anxious to obtain information on the famous Dutch street organs, particularly in view of the fact that these wonderful and fascinating machines are almost unknown in America and are, indeed, pretty much known only to occupants of Holland itself.

There they have enjoyed a rich historical background, and it is fortunate that Mr. Romke deWaard several years ago combined his great interest in the instruments with his literary ability and historical knowledge, and wrote for the benefit of ours and future generations this wonderful story. It has remained for the Vestal Press, however, to expand this treasure-trove of musical nostalgia by making it readable by the English-speaking persons of the World.

It is also indeed fortunate that Mr. Wade Jenkins of Hanover, Massachusetts, an eminent linguist as well as a student of mechanical music became interested in the translation of this work, because he has exercised his unique abilities to put into his efforts all the warmth and affection for the instruments that Mr. deWaard created in his original manuscript. The appreciation of both these men for these wonderful machines will become apparent to the reader.

It should be recognized that this book was written before the great development of interest in researching the history of automatic music that has occurred since 1961, and certain facts have since come to light which tend to disagree with some statements in this text. However, they are certainly minor in character, and we ask the reader to pay them little heed, and to enjoy this great story in the broadest sense.

The mere reading of a book cannot in itself, of course, give the entire story of the complete beauty of any musical instrument — this can only be accomplished when the mind can hear the magnificent sounds of the machines of which the written word expounds. Fortunately, a number of fine sound recordings have been made in recent years of the Dutch street organs, and while they are not often found in ordinary record shops, they can be obtained with little difficulty. At the end of the book is a discography which will help the reader to select fine music which will aid in completing his understanding of why so many persons are putting forth great efforts to preserve this interesting musical heritage.

Harvey N. Roehl
The Vestal Press   1967

Introduction

Imagine a miniature musical instrument as delicate as a cobweb built into a pocket watch, side by side with a monumental Mortier dance organ with a facade measuring eighteen by twenty-seven feet. These are the extremes of a practically endless series of mechanical musical instruments, all of which have in common that they are not played by musicians, but produce music automatically. One could not but feel, as we do, that this would be a most worthy field for musicological research. However, if you were to delve into literature seeking standard reference works about these instruments, you would not have much luck. Besides the works of the famous theorists of the seventeenth and eighteenth centuries, such as Kircher, De Caus, Schott, De Fluctibus, Mersenne, Bonanni, and Engramelle, you would find only three contemporary works dealing with mechanical musical instruments which should be mentioned here.

The first would be the thorough, scholarly Swiss work, "Histoire de la Boite a Musicque et de la Musique Mecanique," by Alfred Chapuis with the cooperation of Louis Cottier, Fredy Baud, P. A. Muller, and Edmond Droz*. The smaller first section of this book deals with mechanical musical instruments in general, and the remainder is devoted to music boxes. The second work is, "Vom Glockenspiel zum Pianola", by Alexander Buchner**, also an excellent and very well documented book, which presents a systematic study of mechanical musical instruments. The lavish format of this book is especially impressive in the numerous splendid illustrations, consisting of photographs of the most beautiful self-playing musical instruments ever

---

* Issues of the Swiss periodical of watches and jewelry, Scriptar's, s.a. Lausanne, 1955.

** Artia, Prague, 1959.

made, drawings, schematics of the mechanisms, and many examples of the music. As far as the text itself is concerned, however, this book is more concise than Chapuis' work. The third book is, "Music Boxes, their Lore and Lure", by Helen Hoke and John Hoke.* It is written in a popular style, mainly concerning music boxes, and only a general and rather sketchy outline is given of other types of automatic instruments. It is particularly appealing because of the long play record it contains, with recordings of twelve music boxes and five other types of machine.

In the study of this literature, three things are striking. In the first place, the remarkable fact presents itself that all three books were published in or after 1955. Furthermore, in none of these books is there any attention paid to the development of street organs during this century. Both Chapuis and Buchner content themselves with a brief survey of the history of the street organ up through the period of Gavioli, in spite of the fact that the evolution of the street organ didn't really get started until after Anselme Gavioli had introduced the book organ in 1892. In fact, the attention which Chapuis pays to the street organ is insignificant compared to the detailed and elaborate manner in which he describes other mechanical instruments (with the exception of reed organs, which he does not mention). In the third place, it is striking that, so far, no Dutch author has ever written a book on mechanical musical instruments. Stranger still, never have any of the capable Dutch musicologists paid any attention at all to the field of automatic musical instruments within the framework of their science. Must we assume that the Netherlands does not share in the revival of interest in these machines which exists in other countries, and, further, that nowhere in the world is there any interest in the street organ as it developed in the course of this century?

---

* Hawthorn Books, New York.

2

Fortunately, neither is the case. On the contrary, interest in mechanical music has very definitely revived also in Holland and, concerning street organs, we can attest to a new wave of sympathy which has risen high in our own country and even spilled over to other lands. Indeed, awakening interest in the pierement (the unique Dutch term reserved for mobile street organs playing book music) had already manifested itself in the years 1952-55 and, as such, preceded the publication of the three foreign books on mechanical musical instruments.

Is it a mere coincidence that the revival of interest in the pierement in our country and in other types of mechanical music in other countries run practically parallel? Probably not. It seems to us that it has something to do with a reaction to the all too technical and mathematical character of our modern, materialistically inclined society, both in Holland and abroad. The ever faster pace of life threatens to rob us of any opportunity of finding solace in the bits of romance and poetry which have been handed down to us by former generations. Is it any wonder that in such a social structure many of us must struggle with feelings of melancholy and nostalgia when our thoughts drift back to that which we have loved in our youth, but for which there is no longer a place in the maelstrom of daily life? And it is not in consequence that one does not yearn for the technically complex but for that which is appealing for its very simplicity, in the satisfaction of musical desires as well as in other things?

Our opinion, then, is that the time is ripe for the appearance of a Dutch book on automatically playing musical instruments, in which special emphasis is laid on barrel organs. We think it is timely and appropriate for the following reasons: there is a desire for a resume of all those details which have any significance about mechanical musical instruments, which could not but prove a foundation, a stimulant, and a point of departure for scientific research in various areas. We think in this connection, of course, principally of musicology. This whole area is still one which is mainly unexplored. Although the works of Chapuis and Buchner made a start at opening up this area, they are still just a beginning, except for music boxes, about which Chapuis was elaborate, as far as we are concerned. The work should be continued. Would it be too optimistic to anticipate that, with the most important data about the development of the various instruments through the years available to them, our musicologists might begin seeking the connection between these data and whatever they themselves might have discovered by dint of their own scientific research? They would in turn give tremendous support to those people who gather documentary material for "The Circle of Friends of the Barrel Organ" (De kring van draaiorgelvrienden) and the museum, "From Music Box to Street Organ" (Van speeldos tot pierement).

Furthermore, by this book we hope to stimulate scientific work in the areas of sociology and psychology. If you do not see the connection between these sciences and automatic musical instruments immediately, let us look at the barrel organ as an example. Are these instruments not a social phenomenon, and would not sociologists seeking an original theme for a thesis feel fortunate if offered material for one? Almost without exception, anyone planning scientific research on a given subject will begin by checking the available literature. If he finds it stimulating enough, he will delve deeper, but if the opposite is true he will choose a different subject. However, will this not also be true if he can find no material at all and so has no point of departure? If a sociologist were to conceive of a thesis on the social aspects of the hand organ, would he not be pleased to find a book setting forth the three ways in which the instruments manifest themselves: as street, fair, and dance organs? The street organs could easily be a point of departure for research into street musicians as a group in society; the fair organs could stimulate research into the sociological implications of fairs in general, and dance organs could trigger research into the attraction which this instrument has for inn visitors, the frequency of visits to establishments with or without organs, etc. In the case of psychology, it is no different. Immediately one thinks of the role automatic instruments can play in satisfying musical desires, particularly for those who either cannot play an instrument themselves or do not have the opportunity to listen regularly to music performed by others, or for those . . . and believe me, there are many . . . who simply prefer a music box or a street organ. What does the love for the pierement mean, scientifically speaking? How is it possible that moods of frustration and dejection can be dispelled in such a harmless and refreshing way by the sentimental, emotional music of the pierement? It is popularly said that a barrel organ can give one a "really good cry." The answer is in the realm of the scientifically trained psychologists. However . . . they will only be able to give the answer when they have accumulated some elementary knowledge about these organs, which this book aims to supply.

Self-playing instruments are certainly worth serious study in Dutch literature. We have already mentioned the enjoyment these machines afford those who either do not play an instrument themselves or cannot depend on music played by others, as well as to those who simply prefer the automatic music of, say, music boxes or organs, especially when they are in a sentimental mood. Moreover, many of these instruments merit our attention because they are the most democratic performers imaginable. The 1956 exhibition at Utrecht, "From Music Box to Pierement," drew more than 14,000 visitors from every level of our society within the eight days of its duration. The twenty-three street-organ competitions organized within the past five years have been again and again a veritable feast for the eyes and ears of the tens of thousands of interested people who have come. The membership roster of the "Circle of

Street Organ Friends" has steadily increased to more than eleven hundred during the six years of its existence. The number of carillons has risen to over one hundred, and they ring out to the enjoyment of the entire community. Cannot we ascribe this same democratic character to our fair organs, dance organs, and orchestrions?

A more penetrating probe of the field of automatic music promises to yield most interesting results. It is striking, in placing side by side instruments played by musicians on the one hand and those played automatically on the other, that the most remarkable extremes and contrasts appear each time in the area of the latter. At the beginning of this introduction, we have already pointed out the droll contrast between a musical pocket watch and a Mortier dance organ. However, not only in mere size, but also in many other respects are diametrically opposed records attained by the mechanically playing instruments, for instance, in volume of sound, in effect on the listener, in the atmosphere in which the instrument is heard, in the character of the music, and in the nature of the mechanism. Imagine, for a moment, the music box hidden in the jewel box of a delicate, aristocratic lady in her intimate boudoir. How subtly does the ethereal tune caress her soul! Now, picture the opposite extreme . . . a mighty Gavioli organ in a steam carousel, captivating the throngs of people with its compelling, irresistible music, or the awesome booming of a great bronze bell, pealing out over the heads of tens of thousands of listeners.

Another remarkable contrast . . . the stately and aristocratic flute clock (Floten-Uhr) which played music of Mozart and Haydn in Patrician drawing rooms became the forerunner of that beloved instrument of the common man: the barrel organ.

This comparison by contrasts can even be carried into the details of construction. Examine the simple mechanism of a canary organ alongside the ingenious and bewildering layout of a large orchestrion with a complete orchestra of automata which play instruments complete with movements of arms, legs, and heads, while the earnestness with which all this is done is reflected in the sparkling movements of their eyes.

Between these extremes lie the many variations of the most divergent kinds of automatic instruments . . . divergent regarding music, exterior, and destination . . . which constitute a rich, romantic, and fascinating genre that so far has been sorely neglected.

We Dutchmen particularly should be the pioneers since the beginning as well as the culmination of the development of mechanical music is in the Netherlands. This evolution began with the music barrel of the automatically playing carillon, which was first applied in the Netherlands and Flanders and still typifies the steeple music of the low lands, and reached its zenith when the building of numerous beautiful book organs was commissioned by some of our concerns. There is no time to lose! A scientific historic survey of the things mentioned in this book or a well-presented documentary would also greatly increase the chances of preserving the many mechanical musical instruments which for the moment still exist but threaten to be lost within a short time if financial help is not soon forthcoming. For only with this help will it be possible to buy these instruments, restore them, and give them a home in the museum "From Music Box to Pierement" or some other appropriate place. On the other hand, losing these instruments could mean losing precious data which would be indispensable for historic research. Let us not underestimate this danger! With the exception of the carillons, none of the types of instruments discussed in part one of this book is being made now. How careful it is necessary to be with the few instruments still remaining of the great numbers of each type once manufactured but now lost, for the most part, simply because, one day, they became old-fashioned. Such was the fate of the flute clocks, the canary organs, the belly-organs (hand organs), the big barrel organs, the barrel pianos, the book pianos, the pianolas, the reed organs, and all kinds of music boxes. It was only recently that a stop was put to this tragic trend by the founding of the museum, "From Music Box to Pierement" at Utrecht,* at this writing still existing only in temporary form. May the publication of this book help to give as many instruments and as much documentary material as possible a definite and safe destination in this museum . . . safe from being dismantled and destroyed, as has unfortunately already happened all too often, or (and again, such a strange contrast) safe from being sold for large sums of money to tourists, to disappear from the land where they belong by virtue of their birth or original destination.

After thus justifying the "why" of this book, we want to explain a little about "what" it is.

First, in chapter one we want to give a universal overview of the different systems according to which the automatically playing instruments function. However, since this book is not meant as a technical work about the actual construction of musical instruments, we shall limit ourselves to the character of the origin of the sound, the way in which it is produced, and the way in which a mechanical instrument differs from the same instrument intended to be played by a musician. In other words: we shall not discuss at length how it is technically possible for the instrument to play at all, but instead, how it is possible that it plays automatically. Thus, you will read how the keyboards or tracker bars of the instruments under discussion are operated, but very little attention, if any, will be devoted to how connection is made with the sound sources (flutes, strings, etc.). We will content ourselves with general statements, which will be more than sufficient for

---

* Now situated in the so-called Chatharijne-convent at the Lange Nieuwstraat 36 at Utrecht, open on Thursday and Friday evenings and Saturday and Sunday afternoons.

music technicians, such as pneumatic, electromagnetic, etc. Enough literature exists on these subjects already. That is why we wish to limit ourselves to the subjects to which not enough justice is done in the existing Dutch literature.

In chapters two through six, we shall give a survey of the historical development of the different kinds of automatically playing instruments. We shall discuss successively the five main groups to be distinguished according to sound source and character of the music: the carillons, the pipe organs up to 1900, the reed organs, the string instruments, and the music boxes. The three chapters on pipe organs, reed organs, and string instruments are fairly brief because from the available data the correct historical development can be deducted only to a limited extent. Therefore, we had to work with the material available and could supply few details in general.

Concerning carillons and music boxes, things are different. However, although there is an extensive literature on these instruments, we felt that these categories should also be treated in the same concise manner to maintain a consistent approach. Referring to already existing literature will answer the needs of those who wish to delve deeper into these subjects.

In part one we limit ourselves to those instruments which were made more or less regularly and which merit attention in the first place as musical instruments. Thus, the instruments which are considered curiosities and in which not the music as such but some other specialty is the raison d'etre will not be considered. At the most these specimens will be mentioned in passing where necessary for the sake of completeness in connection with some other topic under discussion. We think in this case of the dolls which actually play real instruments and which are called "androides" by Buchner.* Therefore, if you wish to know more about the famous flute player of Jacques de Vaucanson, we refer you to what Chapuis and Buchner have written about it. The

* See page 85.

same goes for the androides of father and son Jaquet-Droz, of which the most famous is a girl playing the organ with completely natural movements of her fingers, head, eyes, shoulders, and bosom. While it may be true that others later on have imitated these eighteenth century masters and made similar androides (the last being the American, Cecil E. Nixon, who created a life-size figure of an Egyptian woman, Isis, reclining on a sofa and playing a zither with both hands), still we do not feel justified in calling the androides a kind of musical instrument. At most, not the instruments played but the dolls themselves could be classed as a type. Moreover, the emphasis here is not on the music but on the ingenious way in which the dolls function. We shall also skip the artificially singing birds*, which were manufactured in great quantities in the nineteenth century, for, however true to nature these birds may sing, the sound they produce is not music but only chirping. There is another reason why we limit ourselves. The more concise we are in part I of this book, the more elaborate we can afford to be in part II about the development of the pierement. That we set aside more space for the pierement than we devoted to all the other mechanical musical instruments combined we feel is justified for three reasons: no book has ever been written about the pierement, the pierement is the mechanical musical instrument in which there is the most general interest, and there exist more data about the pierement than could even be incorporated in an elaborately conceived study of the subject. The latter fact is due to the pioneer work done by the members of the "Circle of Street Organ Friends" (1954) in documentation. Although only a few of these pioneers can be mentioned by name within the framework of this book, we are not any the less grateful for these data to the many others without whom the publication of this work would not have been possible.

---

* See Buchner, page 83.

How Do Automatically- Playing Musical Instruments Work?

At the risk of disheartening those readers who thirst after romanticism, we must devote this first chapter to a technical subject which must be set up didactically and which may, therefore, be somewhat abstruse for some readers. However, in order to understand the history of the development of the various types of mechanical musical instruments, one must first have some insight into the manner in which these instruments function in general. This we hope to give you now, so that you may understand the mechanisms of the instruments discussed in chapters two through six. Then it will be possible to identify them briefly each time they pop up, and we shall not find it necessary to interrupt our story each time to explain the technical details.

In order to clarify the difference between mechanical musical instruments and those meant to be played by musicians, we must distinguish between: 1. the sound sources proper of the instruments; 2. the way in which these sound sources are made to vibrate; and 3. the manner in which the instruments are played.

1. Concerning the sound sources, all musical instruments (mechanical ones as well as those played by musicians) are divided into three main groups: the idiophones, the chordophones, and the aerophones.

With the idiophones, the sound is produced by vibrating a series of elastic bodies, each of which has a set pitch. These members are usually made of metal, as in bronze bells, the celeste, the metallophone (steel plates), the tongues or reeds of a harmonium or accordion, and the steel teeth of a music box comb. The members can also, however, be of wood, as in the xylophone, or of glass, as in the bottle register in a bottle organ (page 138) and the glass bells of some curious carillons, such as that in the summer residence of Czar Peter II. The idiophonic sound sources can even be made of porcelain. The latter is the case with the carillon in the tower of the Maria Church in Meissen. For the subject now under consideration, it is of importance to bear in mind that with idiophonic instruments, there must be a separate sound-giving body for each note the instrument is capable of producing. Therefore, the number of sound sources always corresponds to the number of notes in the instrument.

With the chordophonic sound sources, the sound originates from vibrating strings, so we can call this group simply "string instruments." Some of them possess for each note one or more strings. This is the case with the piano and the zither. In other instruments, only a limited number of strings is available and on each of them, a whole series of notes can be produced. This happens because only a part of the string is brought into vibration, a progressively shorter part as the notes go higher and higher. To this latter group belong, among others, all bowed instruments (violin, cello, bass, etc.) and also plucked instruments such as the guitar and the mandolin.

With aerophonic instruments, the sound is created by bringing air columns inside the pipes (flutes) into vibration. These pipes can be made of wood or metal, as it is not the actual pipe but only the air column inside which produces the sound. This is the principal difference from both the idiophonic and the chordophonic types, in which the sound is produced by the vibration of the sound sources themselves.

The aerophonic instruments can be subdivided into instruments having one or more separate sound sources for each note to be produced, and instruments in which all notes are created by one and the same sound source. The first is the case with all kinds of organs, the second, with the wood and brass wind instruments, which are used in a symphony orchestra (flute, oboe, clarinet, bassoon, trumpet, bugle, trombone, tuba, etc.). In the latter instruments, one can produce various notes by vibrating only a part of the air column inside the pipe (here also a shorter part, as the note must go higher), and also by blowing the air into the pipe in different degrees of force, particularly in the brass instruments. Perhaps you are wondering why areophonic instruments could not simply be called "wind instruments." This would not be possible because there are also wind instruments which are not aerophonic, as in the case of the idiophonic reed instruments. This brings us immediately to the next part of our subject: the way in which the sound sources are made to vibrate.

2. Not only in the sound sources themselves, but also in the manner used to excite them to vibration, are the governing principles the same in mechanical as well as in conventional instruments. In both this can be done in four ways: striking, plucking, bowing, or blowing. Most idiophonic sound sources are struck (bells, celeste, xylophone, metallophone, bottles), and a few of the chordophonic ones are (pianos). This striking is usually done by smaller or larger hammers, but with bells, may also be done by clappers (tongues).

Some chordophonic instruments are plucked . . . harp, zither, guitar. In chapter six we shall encounter an exclusively automatic idiophonic instrument which must be plucked, the music box. This plucking action is accomplished by picking up the string (or the steel tooth of the music box comb) momentarily and releasing it immediately afterwards. All other chordophonic instruments are bowed . . . that is, all string instruments which are neither struck nor plucked (violin, cello, bass, etc.). All aerophonic sound sources are blown, as is one category of the idiophonic sound sources, the reeds. The action is accomplished by blowing into the pipes or against the tongues with a constant supply of air under pressure.

3. You may be wondering, after this explanation of the various ways in which sound sources are caused to vibrate, whether it is necessary to investigate how the instruments are played. As far as it concerns those played by musicians, is playing them not the same thing as bringing the sound sources into vibration? In a way, this is the case. However, in playing most instruments, much more than simply striking, plucking, bowing, or blowing is involved. This pertains particularly to those instruments which possess for each note at least one separate sound source. In the case of these instruments, on which we shall now focus our attention, the sound sources are only played by the musician directly in exceptional cases. We could mention the celeste, the xylophone, and the cymbals, which are played with small hammers directly by the musician, the zither, of which all strings are directly plucked, and the mouth organ, of which all notes (reeds) are blown directly. With by far most of the instruments which possess one or more separate sound sources, the playing is done indirectly through some sort of intermediary mechanism, consisting of various parts: a. the parts which are designed to agitate the sound sources by striking, plucking, or blowing; b. the so-called claviers (keyboards or tracker bars), which in one way or another are in communication with the parts mentioned in a and c. The parts mentioned under "c" can be more or less complicated, according to the nature of the instrument, but we shall not go into this any further because we want to give you an opportunity to concentrate all your attention on the claviers, which are of special importance in our study.

The clavier of an instrument can be defined as the series of points from which one can induce sound from the instrument. With instruments playable by musicians, this series of points always consists of keys, of which there are several variations. The ordinary keyboard, of course, with its black and white keys controlling the piano, the organ, the harmonium, etc. is universally known. Adaptations of it are the stick clavier of steeple bells and the button claviers of accordions. Sometimes the claviers do not consist solely of manual keys but also of pedal keys, playable by the feet (organ or carillon). In all cases the function of the keys is the same: when one presses down or strikes a key, the corresponding sound source is caused to speak.

And now we arrive at the cardinal point! Claviers are found not only in musical instruments playable by musicians, such as the piano, church, concert, and theatre organs, carillons, the harmonium, the accordion, etc., but also in mechanical musical instruments. The function is the same, the only difference being that claviers intended for musicians are designed for the hands or feet, while those in automatic instruments must be constructed in a very special way. More about these later . . . now we must point out that there is variation in these claviers from instrument to instrument. The key clavier consists of a row of moveable keys; the air clavier, or tracker bar consists of a series of holes through which air passes, and the electrical clavier consists of a series of electrical points of contact.

Although musicians, no matter what claviers they may be playing, have only to do with keys, where mechanical musical instruments are concerned, we know of two other types of claviers. Moreover, it will become clear that the key claviers of mechanical instruments are played in a different manner than those of "ordinary" musical instruments. However, the definition for "clavier" being a series of points from which the activation of the sound sources may be controlled, this term will still apply for all three kinds of clavier mentioned.

Now, just what do the mechanisms through which the claviers of mechanical instruments are played consist of, and in what way are they played? They function by moving, in a regular tempo, some sort of surface across the clavier, upon which the music is registered in a pattern which enters into communication with the contact points of the clavier. This pattern may consist of elevations which have been mounted on this surface, or of holes being punched in it. The surfaces on which the musical pattern has been registered . . . from here on to be called the "carriers" of these patterns . . . can be: cylinders revolving around their axis, circular-shaped discs revolving around their centers, strips which can be rolled up, and folding cardboard books. With the cylinders and some discs, the music pattern consists of elevations. The former have wire pins and sometimes bridges (two wire pins with a horizontal bridge), and the latter have small punched-out projections or burrs. In the case of other types of disc, as well as in strips and books, the pattern consists of punched holes. The cylinders may be made of wood or metal; the discs are usually of metal, sometimes of cardboard. The strips are mostly of paper, sometimes of harder material, and the books are always of sturdy, stiff cardboard.

Now we shall investigate how the claviers are played by the carriers of the musical pattern. First we must premise that the patterns consisting of elevations can play key claviers exclusively, while those consisting of holes can play both key and air claviers, as well as electrical ones. In the case of the key claviers being played by elevated patterns, the communication is achieved by the wire pins and bridges, or burrs, picking up the keys of the clavier (with metal projections or burrs, also sometimes pushing in or sideways), and releasing them again. In sound sources which must be struck (bells and pianos), or plucked (music boxes, zithers), wire pins or burrs alone are sufficient. The striking or plucking proper only occurs at the moment when the pin releases the key (more about this later in the chapters about carillons and music boxes). In those sound sources which must be blown, bridges as well as pins are needed. The blowing begins at the moment when the key is lifted, which makes the air supply available to the involved flute(s). For the notes which are of short duration, wire pins are sufficient, for these release the keys immediately after reaching the highest point. For longer lasting notes, bridges are necessary which hold the keys up as long as the value of the note indicates. In the key claviers played by "elevated patterns" the pins, bridges or burrs do touch the keys, but the surface of the cylinders or discs does not. The opposite is the case with the key claviers which are played by "hole patterns." The pattern carriers are locked into a clamp mechanism which consists of a lower and an upper part. In the lower part the clavier proper is found, consisting of a series of thin and almost touching metal keys which are pushed up by springs. The upper part of the contrivance can usually be raised and consists in many cases of a brass roller with a series of grooves around its circumference. The number of grooves corresponds with the number of keys in the clavier. When the top is brought down, it can be clasped to the lower part. If this were done without having the pattern carrier in the mechanism, the ends of all the keys would protrude up into the grooves in the roller. If, however, a carrier is in place, all the keys are forced down by it. To withstand this force, only pattern carriers made of sturdy material are used, as a rule . . . that is, books or discs, but usually, no paper strips. When the pattern carrier is moved through the mechanism, the holes punched in it come into position above the appropriate keys, which spring upward through the openings, so that in the new position the ends of these released keys will be protruding into the grooves of the brass roller. They will remain in this position until the holes have passed and the stiff material of the pattern carrier pushes them back down again. In the meantime, you understand, the sound sources have been made to speak at the moment in which the keys spring upward, and they have continued to sound until the keys are forced down again.

The air claviers (tracker bars) and the electrical claviers can be played only by "hole patterns." In practice, these are always punched into books or strips. In air claviers, it is also necessary that the strips or books be sealed tightly against the clavier because the holes in it must be covered tightly. The communication between the pattern and the points of contact of the clavier takes place as follows. Through the holes in the latter, air is being moved under constant pressure. This flow is shut off by the strips or books which form an airtight seal in their passage over the clavier. As soon as holes punched in these carriers appear above the contact points of the clavier, the air is immediately released and can resume its flow, thus sending the impulse to the connected sound source to speak. Books playing air claviers are usually clamped down in much the same way as are books which play key claviers. Where air-claviers are the case, however, there usually is no top and bottom part to the mechanism, but the strips are held against the clavier, or tracker bar, by a system of rolls as indicated in the sketch below.

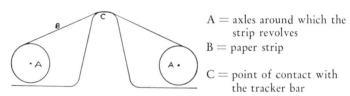

A = axles around which the strip revolves

B = paper strip

C = point of contact with the tracker bar

Of course, the length of the notes is always proportionate to the length of the holes in all air claviers. The electrical claviers also consist of a top and a bottom part, and the books or strips are in contact with both parts as they move along in between. The difference from the key and air claviers is that the books or paper strips do not exert any pressure. In the chapter on carillons we shall go into this more deeply.

In order to give our readers a clear overview of the different ways in which mechanical musical instruments can be played, we shall summarize all the information in a diagram. In the first column the different pattern carriers are arranged, in the second, the type of pattern recorded on them, and in the third, the different claviers played by the corresponding carriers. In the fourth column we have indicated the mechanical musical instruments in which the various combinations of pattern carriers and claviers have been applied in practice. This column will serve as a sort of preview of the subjects discussed in chapters 2 through 6, in which we shall try to give a detailed explanation of the development of the different systems as they appear in the diagram. As you will observe, all the instruments in it function by means of claviers with the exception of cylinder music boxes, in which the sound sources (the teeth of the comb) are directly plucked by the music pattern which is inserted into holes drilled in the cylinder. This arrangement is possible because the teeth of the comb are placed next to each other much like the keys of a clavier and are played in a similar fashion, so here no clavier is necessary. The sound sources themselves are lifted and released again (i.e. plucked) as if they were indeed small keys.

Most of the instruments which you will find in the diagram originated because it was desired to make automatically playable those instruments which were already being played by musicians. In some instances, as in the case of carillons and some kinds of pianolas and harmoniums, the same instruments are playable either manually or automatically. In other cases . . . and this is especially significant . . . the development of mechanical musical instruments led to the creation of completely new instruments which could be played only automatically. This was the case with the music boxes (in which even the sound sources were completely new, see p. 96) and also with the orchestrions and some kinds of street organs, in which various

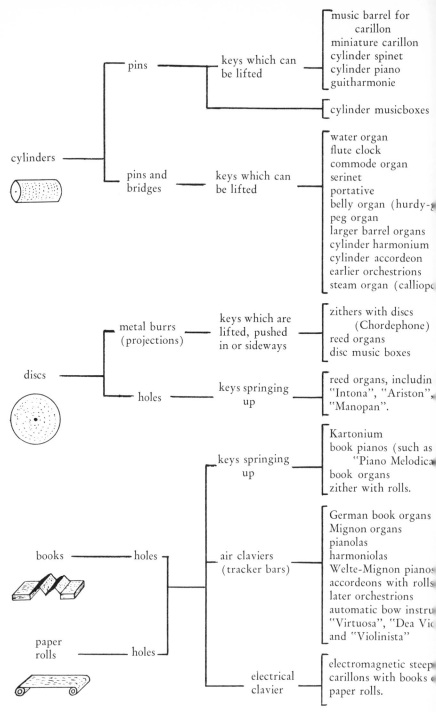

cylinders
- pins
  - keys which can be lifted
    - music barrel for carillon
    - miniature carillon
    - cylinder spinet
    - cylinder piano
    - guitharmonie
  - cylinder musicboxes
- pins and bridges
  - keys which can be lifted
    - water organ
    - flute clock
    - commode organ
    - serinet
    - portative
    - belly organ (hurdy-g
    - peg organ
    - larger barrel organs
    - cylinder harmonium
    - cylinder accordeon
    - earlier orchestrions
    - steam organ (calliope

discs
- metal burrs (projections)
  - keys which are lifted, pushed in or sideways
    - zithers with discs (Chordephone)
    - reed organs
    - disc music boxes
- holes
  - keys springing up
    - reed organs, includin "Intona", "Ariston", "Manopan".

books — holes
paper rolls — holes
- keys springing up
  - Kartonium
  - book pianos (such as "Piano Melodica
  - book organs
  - zither with rolls.
- air claviers (tracker bars)
  - German book organs
  - Mignon organs
  - pianolas
  - harmoniolas
  - Welte-Mignon pianos
  - accordeons with rolls
  - later orchestrions
  - automatic bow instru
  - "Virtuosa", "Dea Vic and "Violinista"
- electrical clavier
  - electromagnetic steep
  - carillons with books
  - paper rolls.

20

sound sources were applied in new combinations which were not found in instruments played by musicians. In this connection, the combination of strings, pipes, xylophone, metallophone and percussion in some kinds of orchestrions comes to mind. As you have seen, all kinds of musical instruments are in the diagram, from the standpoint of sound sources (idiophone, chordophone, and aerophone), as well as the manner in which they made to sound (striking, plucking, blowing, and bowing). The instruments which are bowed are in an exceptional position, for they are the only ones which have no separate sound source for each note. The remarkable thing here is that the automatic bow instruments are still played by means of a clavier, contrary to those played by musicians. How clearly this fact illustrates the vital role the clavier plays in automatic instruments! For, only by devising a playing system utilizing a clavier was it possible to have bowed instruments which could play automatically. Naturally, there were great technical difficulties to be overcome in developing such an unnatural method of playing bowed instruments, which we shall treat at length in chapter five. For the moment we only want to note that self-playing bowed instruments appeared only at the beginning of this century, when automatic control systems had reached a zenith and technological know-how had developed to a high degree.

Must we now come to the conclusion from the foregoing that the development of the mechanical musical instruments . . . apart from music boxes directly played by cylinders . . . remained limited to instruments played by means of claviers? The answer is in the affirmative, if we exclude androides, singing birds, and similar curiosities. The special position of the androides is due to the fact that the musicians themselves have been mechanized, not the instruments. They could therefore be referred to as "robots." Aside from these curiosities, we must state that the construction of automatic musical instruments which did not function by means of a clavier in general brought so many technical difficulties that no mentionable results were obtained. However, the efforts that were made in this direction and the possibility that reed organs were the result will be discussed in chapter four.

Our conclusion must be that the difference between the automatic instruments and those played by musicians is expressed neither in the nature of the sound sources, nor in the way in which these sound sources are eventually made to speak, but only in the way in which the instruments are played. The automatic instruments must always have claviers which can be played by music patterns drawn over them.

The Carillon 2

As far as we can determine, the starting point of the history of the mechanical musical instrument is to be found in the invention of the music cylinder, which made it possible to play carillons automatically. This cylinder, which has played so many carillons on the hour, half hour and even the quarter hour for almost five centuries, was the first application of the principle of the rotating cylinder with pins inserted into it to play the key clavier. They are often so large that one can stand up straight in them, which proves to be a godsend when it becomes necessary to bolt down from the inside the metal notepins which have been inserted into the holes drilled into the drum's surface. The keys of the clavier of the player mechanism consist of metal levers which rotate on their axes. The ends of these levers are just in front of the outside surface of the cylinder, almost touching it. Wires fastened to the other extremity run vertically upwards and are connected higher up in the steeple to the hammers which strike the bells. These hammers rest on flat springs, so that the head just clears the rim of the bell. Now is the time to assert emphatically that in automatic musicworks the bells are always played by hammers striking from the outside, while the carillonneur plays them from a stick clavier which activates the clappers or tongues, striking them from the inside.

When the music cylinder revolves the metal notes fastened to it lift the levers (usually called "lifters") with the result that the wires attached to the other end of these levers are pulled down, thus lifting the hammers. When the cylinder has turned far enough so that the pins release the levers, the hammers fall back. By their weight they overcome the resistance of the tension springs momentarily to strike the bells soundly, but they are immediately brought back to their original position by the springs, in order to clear the balls and let the unmuffled sound ring out. The moment in which the bell is brought to sound almost coincides with the moment the pin releases the lever, except for the time necessary for the hammer to fall. This characteristic is true of all instruments using cylinders in which the sound sources are struck or plucked, such as barrel pianos and music boxes.

The pins are inserted into the holes drilled into the music cylinder in horizontal rows at regular intervals. The distance between the rows amounts to a few centimeters. When new music has to be set up on a carillon barrel, a strip of wood marked with the notes of the bells is placed above the holes so the arranger will know where to place the pins to obtain the correct notes.

The division for noting the music takes place in various ways, depending on whether one has to do with an old

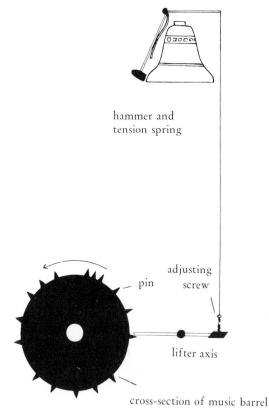

hammer and
tension spring

adjusting
screw

pin

lifter axis

cross-section of music barrel

fashioned cylinder with permanent pins or a new one with adjustable pins, not developed until this century. With the former, the correct measure is found by using pins of various sizes for each beat, half beat and sometimes quarter beat. Let us assume that the distance between two horizontal rows of holes corresponds, for instance, with a 4/4 measure, so that one could subdivide this distance into eight half beats by using pins of eight different lengths. In order to clarify this explanation, we illustrate here the pins for the first, second, third, and fourth beats of such a measure, both as seen from the side and also, from the top.

With a new barrel with adjustable pins, one procedes

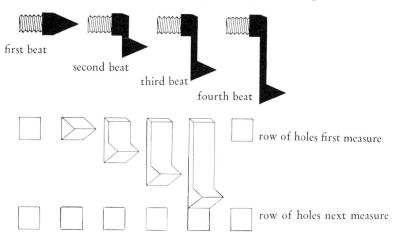

first beat

second beat

third beat

fourth beat

row of holes first measure

row of holes next measure

as follows: the strip with the notes of the bells indicated on it is laid on the clavier. In this case it has been very carefully made and is attached in such a way to the axis of the clavier that it can rotate around it. As will be evident in a moment, in this system the placement of the strip is highly critical for the accuracy of the measures. (With the old type of cylinder this was not the case; with them the strip is mostly laid in the notches of the gear train which drives the cylinder and which is all around it.) When the strip is rested against the cylinder the beginning chord or note is set. Pins with loose screws are used. This screw can be moved back and forth in the groove which is made in the center of the vertical part of the pin. When the screws with the adjustable pins have been put into place in the holes of the barrel, the pins remain on the strip until the screws have all been fastened on the inside of the cylinder, which is then turned so far by means of a dial that the strip comes to the precise spot where the next note or chord must be set. Thus, it is possible to turn the cylinder carefully just so many millimetres as indicated by the music. One can read the measures directly from the dial. This system of determining carefully the desired division into measures by means of an indicator dial is a result of the invention of Engramelle, whom we shall discuss in the chapter on reed organs. At this point, more pins are put in place in the cylinder, which remains on the strip until the screws are tightened, etc.

We have gone rather deeply into the theory of the music cylinder and the pinning of the music, because it is the basis of so many instruments. We hope not only to have given you some insight into the way the music cylinder of a carillon functions, but also to have explained also in general how the music pattern is applied to the cylinder's surface in all instruments working from a cylinder and a key clavier. In one respect, the carillon barrel differs from most other cylinder instruments, however. With the carillon, not every key of the clavier sounds a different sound source. Many bells have not just one, but sometimes two or three hammers, each corresponding to a separate lifter. In this way it becomes possible to strike the same bell twice or more in quick succession. This is not possible with a bell with only one hammer, because a certain amount of time is necessary for the key of the clavier to raise the hammer when the wire pin passes underneath. Within this time, the hammer cannot possibly strike the bell twice. However, when a bell has two hammers, they can be lifted at any given moment in very quick succession, and since the second one has already been lifted when the first falls, it can be immediately released so the result is two quickly repeated notes. But let us not forget that the readers who are historically inclined must be satisfied in this chapter. First, we want to discuss the origin of the music cylinder.

Until 1925, it was assumed by bell experts that the music cylinder was invented in or around 1481 by Bartholomeus van Koecke, a watchmaker from Aalst. Mr. A. Loosjes, one of the pioneers to whom we owe a revival of interest in the art of the carillon about the time of the first world war after the famous carillonneur, Jef Denijn, had awakened new interest in the bells in Flanders, writes in his standard reference work* the following on the subject: "Some say that the carillon was invented in 1481." This is not correct; it was already in existence at that time. But B. van Koecke at Aalst, a man who, according to some, was not quite in his right mind, seems to have invented the music barrel in 1481, allowing one to hear any given melody, much as we know it today. We also should like to acquaint you with the following passage which Mr. Loosjes quotes in this regard from Fetis' "Biographie universelle des musiciens": "Koecke, founder of bells at Aalst during the second half of the fifteenth century invented the carillon in 1481, according to Ortelius, quoted by Gramaye. He was the first one to conceive the mechanism of the notated cylinder for ringing the bells and forming melodies. Ortelius says that he was a man with very little sense, but the invention of such a complicated mechanism indicates extraordinary creative power. These words of the famous Antwerp geographer could be explained by the stories to be heard from the inhabitants of Aalst to the effect that Koecke, although certainly a genius in his own right, went to pieces if he encountered unexpected obstacles. His wife, Pharaide, waas supposed to have had great strength of character and so to have lent stability

---

* De toren muziek in de Nederlanden, page 10.

to Koecke in his moments of weakness. According to Belgian sources, the carillon of De Koecke, installed in the bell tower of Aalst, was heard for the first time on Christmas day (December 25, 1487), five minutes before the tower bell sounded noon."

Unfortunately, we shall have to question the authenticity of all this. The theory that Van Koecke invented the music cylinder has been fairly well discredited by the research of the bell specialist, Dr. G. van Doorselaar, who came to the conclusion in his "Legends in the History of Bells" [1] that automatic music installations existed already before 1481, and, further, that there possibly never was a Van Koecke.

In any case, we may accept as a well-documented fact that music cylinders were being constructed as early as the 15th century. Andre Lehr, who showed himself to be a conscientious historian in his work, "The Bell Founders Francois and Pieter Hemony," [2] written on the occasion of the Hemony Memorial Year, 1959, has added the weight of his testimony in support of this view. These very early specimens were in the form of metal strips placed inside rings. Later these developed into a simple cylinder. It was quite natural that automatic music for carillons should lead to similar applications in other instruments along the path we have been tracing, for around the 15th century the towns in Flanders and the Netherlands flourished more and more. The soaring, dignified towers of these towns came to be a kind of symbol of the pride and love of liberty of the citizens; a symbol both visible and audible from a great distance, the latter due to the large bells suspended within. Even at this point there was a distinction being made between tolling bells, rung on certain solemn occasions, or to warn the citizens of fire, flood, or other immi-

---

1. "The Art of Bellplaying", acts of the 2nd congress, 's-Hertogenbosch 1925, pages 157-158.

2. Published by B. Eysbouts, C. V. Asten.

The Westertoren at Amsterdam. The hammers of the mechanical carillon may be seen arranged outside the bells.

29

nent disaster, and striking bells, which were used to announce the time of day, the appropriate number of blows of the hammer corresponding to the hour.

Particularly in the southern part of the Netherlands, a desire for display and ceremony led to the development of smaller, lighter sounding bells to serve as accompaniment or setting for the huge, ponderous striking bell, and thus a third category of bells was created, the music bells. These small bells were called "voorslag," because of the fact that they were heard before the clock struck the hour, or "appeelkens," because they called for your attention to the hour to be struck. A late-Latin term, "quadrillionem", which was also applied to them and from which the word "carillon" is derived, indicates that the common number of these music bells must have been four. However, the number was gradually extended to ten or twenty in the course of the fifteenth and sixteenth centuries. But how could it be arranged to play melodies on these bells, rather than random notes? Would it be necessary to have a man stationed in the tower to play them day and night on the hour and half hour? Of course, this was not practicable and a different solution would have to be found. We owe our present enjoyment of automatic musical instruments to the fact that this need resulted in the invention of the music cylinder when inventive minds were applied to the problem. First, the invention of the music cylinder led to the subsequent development of all other automatically playing musical instruments. In the second place, it furnished a stimulus for the evolution of the sphere of the carillon, which was to have such significance for the musical culture of the Dutch and the Flemish. How did this come about? First, this invention made it possible to have actual melodies played automatically on the bells, which in turn created a demand for a larger repertory of melodies than could be performed on the few bells of the original "voorslagen." The more bells one has, the larger the number of available notes, and the more different melodies that can be played. Furthermore, the more bells there are, the more interesting one can make the arrangements of the melodies to be pinned on the music cylinder. When the number of bells began to be increased for these reasons, there was another and even more important result: Now it became worthwhile to make the carillon playable by means of a stick carillon personally by a carillonneur. Another new perspective was opened in the art of bell-playing, and we have an excellent object lesson on the far-reaching effects an automatic musical instrument may have on the development of music.

Since it would be out of perspective to attribute too much significance to the art of bell playing, suffice it to say that the technique continued to develop until well into the 17th century, after the invention of the music barrel and the stick clavier. In that century the zenith was reached, primarily due to the famous bell founders, Francois and Pieter Hemony and their brilliant advisor, the blind bell player from Utrecht, Jhr. Jacob van Eyck. Unfortunately, in the 18th and especially, the 19th centuries, the art of the carillon deteriorated, but in our own time it has again come to flourish to a hitherto unknown extent, both in the art of founding and tuning and in the actual playing. The Dutch foundries are famous the world over, and never have bells been cast of such purity, perfection, and richness of tone as during the past few years. Our advice to all civic and church boards, or anyone else concerned, is: if you are thinking of a set of bells, don't wait any longer! Order it now! Anyone wishing more information about carillons or the training of carillonneurs, as it was originally given only in Mechelen, but since 1953 has also been at the Netherlands School for carillonneurs at Amersfoort, should contact the board of the Netherlands Carillon Association.[1] If you need a carillonneur, you can turn to the same association for advice and information. The magazine,

---

1. Secretary H. E. B. Warnaars, Oude Zijds Voorburgwal 101, Amsterdam.

"Klok en Klepel," (Bell and Clapper) is published annually by the Netherlands Bell Playing Association, and gives news of all happenings and developments in the field of bells. As additional reading on the development of the art of bell playing, we can recommend the booklet, "Luid-klokken en Beiaarden in Nederland", (Tolling bells and Carillons in the Netherlands) by Ferdinand Timmermans.[1] At this point we only wish to reaffirm that it was an automatically playing musical instrument incorporating a music cylinder which made this development possible.

The steeple carillon as it developed after the invention of the music barrel was by its very nature a musical instrument of and for the whole nation. It was of course impossible to enjoy such an instrument in the intimate atmosphere of the living room of a private individual who might wish to own one. This kind of demand could only be met when clockmakers began making miniature carillons so small that they could be used in or on time-pieces for the home. The mechanism of these miniature carillons was in principle the same as that of these built for a tower. The pins, of course, were much smaller and were inserted into holes drilled in small, solid cylinders. Their music was performed on very small replicas of full-size bells, or on dome-shaped bells much like our present bicycle bells. As early as the 17th century this type of clock with miniature carillon was being made, primarily in Flanders, Northern France, and England. One of the oldest specimens still in existence belongs to the collection of Th. Beyer in Zurich. It has nine bells cast in true bell shape and mounted on top of the clock in much the same way bells were suspended in a tower at that time. It bears the signature, Jean Dubois. Another very old miniature carillon, in which the music is played by 13 dome-shaped bells, is in the Science Museum in London. We can also admire a similar clock in the museum "From Music Box to Pierement". The manufacture

---

1. Heemschutserie, deel 33, Allert de Lange, Amsterdam, 2nd printing, 1950.

of these clocks with miniature carillons constituted the second phase in the history of mechanical musical instruments, and they are the link between the music barrel and the Floten-Uhr (flute clock), which we shall discuss in the next chapter.

But we must return briefly to the carillons in our bell towers to call attention to a remarkable contrast between the subsequent development of the automatic carillon on one hand and all the other mechanical musical instruments on the other. Although in the case of the latter, the cylinder system was replaced by discs, books, or paper rolls during the second part of the 19th century, the original cylinder persisted in the carillon until 1941, or approximately four and a half centuries. It was not until 1941 that A. H. van Bergen, a bell founder at Heiligerlee, applied a new system for the first time to the carillon being built for the new municipal building at Hoogeveen, which constituted an electromagnetic system played by books. After the second world war, the founders Eysbouts at Asten and Petit and Fritsen at Aaalr Rixtel decided to adopt the electromagnetic system, although they chose music patterns cut into strips of strong material instead of the folding cardboard books which are still being used by Van Bergen.

The contacts in electrical claviers are usually made by keys. In the book system of Van Bergen, they are located in the lower portion of the clavier and spring up through the perforations, as in street organs. In the latest system of Eysbouts, which has been utilized of late by Petit and Fritsen, the keys are in the top part of the clavier. By their own weight they drop into the perforations in the strips and in so doing, make the required contact with the terminals in the bottom section of the clavier. We want to stress, however, the difference between the keys of ordinary claviers and those in the electrical ones. In the former type, it is the actual movement of the keys that counts, for that is what activates the sound source, whether mechanically or pneumatically. The motion of the key is in this case indispensable. However, in electrical claviers, the completion of the circuit between the upper and lower points of contact is what is essential. This can be accomplished in other ways than by keys. For example, a few years ago Eysbouts developed a system in which a brush of fine copper wires was placed in the upper part of the clavier. The contacts were made when these wires touched the terminals in the lower part of the clavier through the perforations in the roll. The explanation for the lag in switching from barrels to books or rolls in the carillon, as compared with the other types of instrument, probably lies in the following circumstances: To begin with, little attention was paid to the automatic playing arrangements of the carillon in general because the art of bell playing had deteriorated to such an extent during the 19th century. Then, the need for an extensive repertory is less in the carillon than in other automatic instruments. It has been found that people prefer to hear the same melodies on the hour and half hour, and so it suffices to change them once or twice a year. Even when interest in the area of the carillon . . . including automatic ones . . . was reborn in the course of this century, it still was not possible simply to substitute discs, rolls, or books as they were applied to other instruments, for the great barrels of the carillons. This was due to the fact that much greater force was required to raise the heavy hammers which would strike the bells than was required for the functioning of other mechanical instruments. And, conversely, it is also remarkable to note that the electromagnetic system of the carillon was not applied in other instruments, either. Even when the factory of De Cap at Antwerp built automatic organs with electronic sound sources after the second world war, they still used pneumatic tracker bars.

Regarding the debate concerning which system is the best, opinions vary widely in the world of the bells. Many bell players remain faithful to the old cylinder. They and other advocates of the original system point out that a cylinder installation is stronger and less subject to wear and tear than an electromagnetic one. The bell founders, however, enthusiastically prefer the modern system. In practice, therefore, a modern apparatus is almost always provided with the new carillons, except in cases where music cylinders still exist belonging to bells which were lost during the second world war and which are being replaced by new ones. We take sides with the new system. If they are taken care of by the bell player and an electrician, better results are obtained with less expense from an electric system. We think in this regard specifically of the exact rhythm and the simultaneous sounding of different notes of which chords are made up. With cylinders, it often happens that the hammers do not strike the bells at precisely the right moment, or, in the case of chords, simultaneously, because the pins are not of the same length for various reasons, or they are not at right angles to the barrel. Small differences can easily lead to annoying irregularities. This also goes for the length of the wires with which the lifters are connected to the hammers, and for the resiliency of the springs upon which the hammers rest. When this spring is stronger the hammer will strike the bell with less force and somewhat later than it will with a weaker one. In any case, practice has shown that a very fast scale in, for example, 32nd notes, can ordinarily not be played with precision by a cylinder, while it can be executed perfectly electrically. Furthermore, much less space is required for the new apparatus than for the cumbersome and heavy barrels. Another important advantage of electromagnetic installations is that at any time a new roll or book can be inserted. For instance, during the visit of foreign dignitaries, national tunes or folk songs could easily be programmed on the bells. During St. Nicholas time (December 5) appropriate tunes can be played, and at Christmas time, Christmas tunes, etc. One can also change the tunes played for the hour and the half hour. In this case, the melodies are punched right after each other in rolls or books with the ends fastened together.

When one has heard the tunes a number of times they become etched on the brain and one can tell the time in this way. Another advantage is that the books or rolls can be kept indefinitely. In order to give our readers a picture of the manner in which the various types of self-playing installations are spread out over our country, we shall give a broad survey of a number of the important Dutch carillons at different periods in our history. However, we certainly do not pretend to be complete. Even if we were, our list would soon be outdated because, fortunately, new sets of bells are constantly being manufactured. Carillons dating back to the 16th century and functioning by means of music cylinders are at the Rijksmuseum at Amsterdam and at Edam and Monnickendam, and almost all the famous Hemony carillons (dating from 1644-1678) such as the Westertoren bells, those of the Oudekerkstoren, Zuidertoren, Munttoren and Nicolaitoren at Utrecht, the Sint-Pancrastoren and the Drommedaris at Enkhuizen, and the bells in the Sint-Lebuinustoren at Deventen, the Nieuwetoren at Kampen, the Nieuwe Kerk at Delft, the Onze-Lieve-Vrouwetoren (Long John) at Amersfoort, the Sint-Bavokerkat Haarlem, the Martinitoren at Groningen, the Sint-Janskerk at Gouda and the municipal building at Den Bosch. Most of these Hemony bells have been restored since 1945 and their range extended with series of smaller bells from Dutch foundries, like many other carillons mentioned here. In the towers (toren) mentioned the original music cylinders were all maintained. This will also be done with the Hemony bells of the Sint-Laurenstoren at Rotterdam, the tower at Weesp of the same name, and the municipal building at Maastricht which are now being restored and expanded. It was only in the restoration of the Hemony carillon at Middelstum that the old music barrel was replaced by an electromagnetic clavier with music strips. This will also be done with the Hemony carillon of the Cathar-

Music drum with movable pins in the tower of the Nieuwe Kerk at Delft.

inatoren at Brielle. Other carillons playing from cylinders are those of Melchior de Haze at Alkmaar dating from 1686-1688 (Waagtoren and Grotekerk), Gorinchem and the Hague, and, from the period 1770-1790, those of Andreas van den Gheyn at Schoonhoven, Nijkerk, Schiedam, and Goes. Of the bells manufactured for our country by the English foundries of John Taylor and Gillet and Johnston in the period from 1911-1945, only a few are left, most of them having been stolen during the period 1940-1945. The most important English carillons which were saved, those of the Sint-Jans cathedral at 's-Hertogenbosch, the Onze-Lieve-Vrouwetoren ("Pepper Pot") at Zwolle and the Sint-Plechelmustoren at Oldenzaal, still are operating with the original music cylinders. The Taylor carillon at Appingedam was the only one supplied with a modern clavier and books when it was restored and enlarged in 1959. In many carillons which were made after the war by Dutch founders to replace the stolen English ones, the original music cylinders were again put to use. This was done at Winschoten, Hoorn, Bergen op Zoom, Almelo, Enschede, Breda, Vught, Helmont and the Leiden municipal building. With the exception of the cylinder-operated new carillon of the Cuneratoren at Rhenen, no new cylinders have been made since the war.

Finally we shall mention a number of carillons dating from the period 1941-1960 to which electromagnetic systems have been applied. Van Bergen's book system was used in the carillons at Hoogeveen, Meppel, Nijmegen, Dordrecht, Dokkum, Schagen, Veendam, Ten Boer and Hattum. Strip systems by Petit and Fritsen were used at Heusden, Hulst, Joure, Assen, Gennep, Venlo, Kuijk, Boxmeer, Aarle-Rixtel, and in the Gerardus-Majellakerk and the Jaarbeurstoren at Utrecht. Strip systems of Van Eijsbout are to be found at Middelburg, Vlaardingen, Valkenswaard, Beverwijk, Zeist, IJsselstein, Bolsward, Groenlo, Zevenaar, Sluis, Emmeloord, and the radio carillon in the town hall tower at Hilversum.

38

Pipe Organs 3

Of the five main categories of mechanical musical instruments which we divided according to kind of music (carillons, pipe organs, reed organs, string instruments, and music boxes), the group of the pipe organs, in which music is produced by automatically blowing into the pipes, is definitely the most important one. To this group belong not only the most interesting and historically valuable old mechanical musical instruments about which we shall speak in this chapter, but also those larger ones which have evolved from them, dating from the end of the 19th century and into the 20th, to which we shall devote the entire second half of this book, the street, fair, and dance organs.

Presumably the history of self-playing pipe organs began with the so-called water organs to be found as early as the 16th century in Italian parks, such as the Villa d'Este at Tivoli near Rome, and the house of cardinal Pietro Aldobrandini near Frascati. These instruments owe their name to the manner in which they were played. This was done by having water spill onto a wheel continuously and "with great force" as we read in the "Journal de voyage" by Montaigne in 1580-1581. This stream of water caused a wheel to turn, moving the pumping rods of the bellows and also turning the cylinder assembly. Thus, by the turning of the wheel the instrument functioned in much the same way as the street organs would a few centuries later. In a sense, the the water organ was already a street organ, although it was not turned by the muscle power of an organ grinder. As far as that goes, the use of hydraulic power is not new. It was already being used to pump the bellows of ordinary organs centuries ago, labor which was later performed by so-called "organ-treaders" and later yet, by motors. A picture of a similar water organ is found on a sarcophagus discovered in Alexandria and dating back to the first century A. D.

Whatever we know about mechanically playing water organs, we owe mostly to the works of the four well-known 17th century theorists, Samuel de Caus, pater Athanasius Kircher, pater Kaspar Schott and Robertus de Fluctibus. The works of de Caus ("Raisons de forces mouvantes," 1615) and Kircher ("Musurgia Universalis," 1650) describe clearly the workings of the water organ and illustrate with drawings, one of which we reproduce here. The proportions are obviously not accurate. The symbolism of the satyr playing the flute and the nymph playing the organ is especially interesting. Could this be a parallel to the difference in character between two such contrasting registers? We also reproduce at this time the music of the round which, according to Kircher, was played by the satyr and the nymph.

For those who would like to study more thoroughly the work of the theorists mentioned above, we give here the title of the work of pater Schott, "Magiae universalis

'An automatic organ machine which utters the voices of animals and birds', according to A. Kircher.

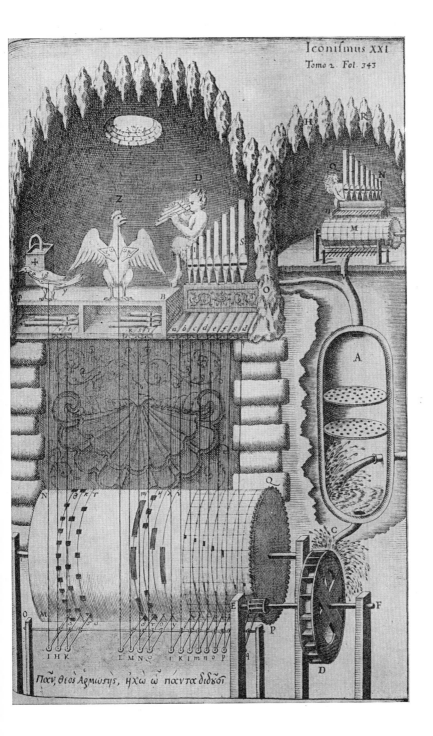

Παν, θεὸς Ἀρμονίης, ἠχῶ ᾧ πάντα διδ̃ςῖ.

naturae en artis," 1657, and that of R. de Fluctibus, "De Naturae Simia", 1618.

Of the many water organs which must have existed at that time, only one, so far as we know, is still preserved, namely the one in the famous mechanical theatre at Hellbrunn, five miles from Salzburg. Shortly before this book went to press, we heard that the English organist, Lady Susi Jeans, had been making an elaborate study of this subject and found that water organs, although Italian in origin, were found in other countries also, namely, England and Holland. Because there was not time to get in touch with this musicologist, we are not prepared at this time to state precisely when, where, and by whom the oldest known water organs were made. We cannot even be sure that the oldest automatically playing pipe organs were indeed water powered. Buchner mentions as the oldest mechanical organs not the Italian water organs, but the organs built in Augsburg also in the 16th century. He cites the city of Augsburg as the "Cradle of the Development of Automatic Organs".[1] Buchner mentions in this regard the organs which were made, commissioned by Emperor Rudolph II, by the Augsburg organ builders K. Eisenburger and G. Henlein in cooperation with the composer-organist Hans Leo Haszler (1564-1612), who composed music for these organs. Buchner derives his data from two lawsuits in which Haszler became involved because of his cooperation with the abovementioned organ builders. But does this prove that the first mechanical organs were made at Augsburg? After all, it is known that at the same time water organs existed in Italy! Possibly stronger substantiation for Buchner's opinion lies in the fact that as early as 1502 Bishop Leonhard von Keutschach commissioned the building of the so-called

_____

1. See page 59.

42

"Hornwerk" for city of Salzburg. The first description of this unusual organ (which was restored repeatedly but, fortunately, was preserved), however, dates from the middle of the 18th century. It would be rewarding to do more research on the history of this "Hornwerk", which is popularly called the "Salzburg Bull".

The automatic organs built by Augsburg builders described by Buchner are all built into objets d'art. Three of them date from the end of the 16th century. In the art museum in Vienna are displayed a beautifully gilded warship with crew (1585) and a building with front steps, balcony, and a stage with gilded sculptures. The third piece, a creche dating from 1589 by Hans Schlottheim was lost in a bombing raid in the second world war.

From the beginning of the 17th century are the "Triumphal Chariot" and the "Tower of Babel" in the Mathematisch-Physikalischer Salon in Dresden. Automatic pipe organs were built into all these pieces, but the number of pipes was generally low and the emphasis was always on the objet d'art and its aesthetic aspect. As a curiosity it also made music. The most famous of these valuable pieces was certainly the "Pomeranian Chest", built by Achilles Langenbucher. It was commissioned by the duke Philips II of Pomerania and, upon its completion in 1617, it was transferred to the duke with much festivity. It was only during the 18th century that manufacture began of different types of automatically playing pipe organs meriting attention primarily as musical instruments. We shall begin with the ones which were built into large floor clocks, and which we shall henceforth call by the usual German name, "Floten-Uhr", since a Dutch equivalent is lacking. The "Floten-Uhren", or flute clocks, were built with a cylinder and a key clavier like the water organs, and probably originated as counterparts of the miniature carillons made by the same clockmakers. Among the oldest and most famous of these clockmakers were the father and son Jaquet-Droz who created during the mid-eighteenth century, among other marvels, the famous clock called the "Berger" (shepherd) because of the flute-playing shepherd seated on top.

The works of a flute-clock.

Besides the shepherd and other animated figures like dolls, a dog, and a bird, some of which also produce sound, there are sets of bells and metal flutes in this masterpiece.

44

This combination of bells and metal flutes we also find in other 18th century clocks, some of them Dutch. Nowadays when we speak of a Floten-Uhr, we mean primarily those instruments which were made in great numbers until approximately the middle of the 19th century in the Black Forest, Geneva, Neuchatel, Dresden, Vienna, and Berlin, and which produced their music from wooden flutes with a soft, subtle quality. This use of wooden pipes brings us another step closer to the music of the street organs and orchestrions. Often the Floten-Uhren were provided with a small group of playful animated dolls who walked tightropes, swung on a trapeze, played musical instruments, etc. Some famous builders of Floten-Uhren were Christian Mollinger, clockmaker to Friedrich Wilhelm II; Primitivus Nemec, librarian to Nicholas Esterhazy; and the Viennese instrument makers J. A. Hoyer, J. Janisch, and the Maelzel brothers.

The movement of a Floten-Uhr was powered by a heavy weight which had to be wound up. In large hall clocks having both chime and cylinder mechanisms, there are three such weights, one for the clock, one for the chime, and one to power the cylinder and bellows of the pipe organ. The latter is always the heaviest by far.

In the introduction we have already stated that the street-organ need not be ashamed of its origin . . . it has excellent ancestry indeed. The Floten-Uhr, which could be considered the grandfather of the street organ, was a very dignified musical instrument and was designed for the rich. Indeed, such famous composers as Haydn and Mozart did not think it at all beneath their dignity to compose special music for these and other drawing-room instruments, usually commissioned by royalty, the nobility, and other such illustrious people. We call your attention in this regard to 31 works by Haydn published by W. Ernst-Fritz Schmid at Gershoven (near Augsburg). Even more important, however, are the three works which Mozart composed for mechanical organ, the Fantasy in F, K. 594, Fantasy in F, K. 608, and Andante in F, K. 616. If you should ever visit the Mozarteum at Salzburg, you may admire the original manuscript of this Andante, of which we reproduce the first few measures here.

We must not neglect to mention that these three works, which Mozart wrote between the end of 1790 and the middle of 1791, the last year of his life, must be classified among the most beautiful and interesting of his creations. They were to be, as G. de Saint-Foix expressed it, his musical testament. This applies in particular to the second Fantasy, K. 608, written on March 3, 1791, which has also been arranged for standard pipe organ by Marcel Dupre and thus has become part of the repertoire of many church organists. G. de Saint-Foix characterizes the work as "a fantasy in the style of the masters, very strict, and displaying the masterful daring and the harmonic liberties of a Bach who might have lived during the last years of the 18th century."

The mechanical organs for which Haydn and Mozart composed were not all Floten-Uhren in the true sense of the word, but consisted also of instruments containing ranks of wooden pipes like those of the Floten-Uhr, and playing from cylinders and key claviers, but built into beautiful cabinets or commodes instead of clock cases. As a result of the much greater available space, these organs were usually much larger and more complete instruments. The period in which these cabinet organs were made constituted the zenith of the genre, the years 1760-1840, for the industry of the expensive pipe organs succumbed to the rapidly expanding new industry of music boxes and reed organs. The self-playing pipe organs were built into other pieces of furniture as well. In the national museum at Prague there is one built into a desk which dates from 1774 built by S. J. Truska, and the "Musee des arts decoratifs" in Paris has one in its collection built into a large mirror.

Whatever may have been the strength of the bond between these pipe organs we have been examining and our present-day pierement (street organs), they were not true hand organs in the sense that they could be operated with a wheel or crank. The first instruments which fit this description were the canary organs, or serinettes, dating from the early 18th century. They were usually tiny instruments, approximately the size of a large model cigar humidor. Their music was very thin and high, because it was produced by only 10 tiny lead pipes tuned to c, d, e, f, g, a, bb, b, c, and d in the four and five-lined octave. Besides the case and the handle, these organs consisted of a wooden drive shaft assembly which was attached to the handle and pumped the bellows, a wooden cylinder studded with pins and bridges, a clavier with 10 keys activated in the usual manner by the cylinder, and finally the ten flutes themselves, their valves controlled directly by the keys of the clavier. The cylinder was shaped like a toothed wheel at one end and driven by a wooden worm gear which fitted into it, the worm being an integral part of the drive shaft assembly. What it amounts to is that the serinette is the least complicated form of the works of all cylinder organs.

If you should wish to study this arrangement, it would be best to acquire a serinette and examine its mechanism first hand. Not all canary organs were limited to only ten pipes . . . larger ones were built with not only one register, but three, all consisting of lead pipes: a two foot (the same pitch as the very small versions), a four foot (an octave lower), and an eight foot (another octave lower). These three registers could be played separately or in any desired

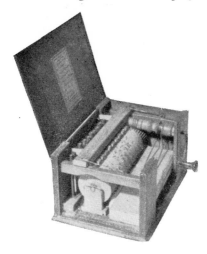
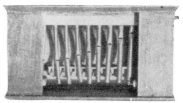

The works and front view of a canary organ, or serinette.

combination. The large canary organs were called "serinette-pionne" in France. The music of all the bird organs was for only one voice, as they were designed to teach melodies to caged birds, or, as Bilderdijk expressed it:

> "The clever finch must train his throat
> To match the organ's every note."

The museum "From Music Box to Pierement" has made quite a name for itself, not only as a museum, but also as a haven for tired and listless songbirds. If you want to verify with your own eyes and ears the beneficial effects of the serinette on a temperamental canary, visit the museum. You will see a canary sitting in a pretty cage, showing absolutely no signs of any zest for life. However, as soon as one of the serinettes is played, the bird starts to warble, making happy, playful movements of its head and beak, and tail . . . so naturally that very few perceive that this creature is just one more of the automatic musical curiosities of the museum. Because the canary organs were handcranked and were mostly made at Mirecourt (Vosges, near Nancy), they were the beginning of an industry which would grow during the 19th century and eventually lead to the building of the most colossal automatic organs that ever existed: the street, fair, and dance organs.

But how is it possible that the bird organ, a tiny drawing-room instrument, evolved into something to play in the street? The explanation is fairly simple from the standpoint of the unschooled street musician. However, to follow the psychology behind this development, we shall have to know something about street music in general. To begin with, we owe its very existence to the fact that there have been individuals since the middle ages and even earlier, who have possessed on the one hand great musical talent and on the other, a strong sense of adventure and a compelling feeling for poetry and romance. Such musicians, thirsting after romance and adventure have been known in all walks of life. On the higher plane, they generally became singers and composers, or sometimes well-known poets. A large part of our folk music we owe to them. The troubadours who existed in France and Spain as early as the 12th and 13th centuries and their German counterparts, the Minnesanger, come to mind. But do not forget that they performed primarily at court and had to do only with the upper class. Simpler musicians who were not qualified for such elevated patronage had to be satisfied with singing their songs in the open for anyone willing to listen, in other words, the populace as a whole! And thus, they moved from place to place, singing and making music and finding their happiness simply in so doing, and also in having complete freedom to go wherever they pleased. (Is this not also true of the street musicians of our own time?) But they always had one obstacle to contend with. If they wanted to bring music which would really caress the ears of their audiences, they had to be capable of playing an instrument themselves, to provide an accompaniment for their own songs or those of their companions. In order to do this, whether on a zither or a lute, a certain dexterity was essential. It goes without saying that there have always been individuals who have made this type of music their career while lacking the capacity to master even the minimum essentials of the art of playing an instrument. It is understandable that they would consider it a godsend to discover an organ so small and light it could be carried under the arm, from which sweet music could be lured, merely by cranking a handle, to accompany their songs. In a picture dating from 1722 we see an Italian street musician carrying under his arm what must be a serinette, judging from its small size. Many street musicians who used similar organs came from Italy. Since they could be carried under the arm, these instruments were ordinarily called "portatives". Thus it came about that the manufacturers of canary organs began making this kind of portative also, for the street musician trade. The fact that the portatives became larger and larger is no cause for wonder, for the street musicians soon came to realize that they needed stronger and fuller sounding music than a portative could furnish. Imagine a

---

Lady with canary organ (end of 18th century).

50

sonorous, virile male voice accompanied by such piping, chirping toots as are typical of bird organs! One cannot but smile at such a disparity. However, there was only one way possible to make the music of the organs stronger and of lower range . . . they had to be constructed with more and larger pipes, which would in turn necessitate a stronger air supply, furnished by larger bellows. In other words, the manufacturers would have to start turning out larger street organs in place of the tiny portatives. This came about, and thus we see that the desire of the musicians themselves for a greater and more nearly normal volume of sound furnished a significant stimulus for the building of larger street organs. The first phase in the subsequent development was that the new instruments were larger and heavier and thus had to be carried by a strap around the neck so that they now hung in front of the abdomen instead of under the arm . . . a fact which led to a new name, the "buikorgel", or belly organ.

In the buikorgel mostly wooden pipes were used, the smaller ones placed vertically in front of the cylinder. The large bass flutes were often placed horizontally in the bottom of the organ case, in order to put to good use the room available underneath the cylinder. The highest and most penetrating of tonal quality were the "Pan flutes", or piccolo pipes, which were always exposed to view in the front of the organ. These were provided with graceful, acorn-shaped finials which also served for the tuning of the pipes.

Oldest known picture of a street organ grinder with a portative, 1722 A. D.

Organo Portatile

Harmonipan buikorgel, 19th century.

Frederik de Meerleer describes the tone of these pipes, the most typical of the buikorgel, as follows: "Pan flutes sounded shrill, happy, lively and, in a certain sense in spite of their sharpness, melancholy . . .".[1]

The buikorgel was among the props used by groups of musicians who presented tableaux on the streets and in the squares, illustrating the story with a large poster divided into sections, usually numbering nine or sixteen, in which were painted in gaudy colors all kinds of dramatic and highly imaginative events. These were sometimes based on actual occurrences like the quintuple murder in the illustration, and sometimes they were strictly fantasies, as long as they were frightening! This type of thing grew out of the craving for sensationalism which existed during the highly romantic second half of the 19th century, when

1. "The Pierement", April 1958.

the tendency was to express feelings and emotions freely. The street musicians furnished an ample outlet for this desire! While one member of the company pointed out the different episodes with a stick, another would sing the story in as many verses as there were episodes to be admired. All these verses, then, were sung to the same recurring melody, whose length coincided with the circumference of the cylinder in the buikorgel which accompanied him. After each verse, the melody would start anew because the cylinder had accomplished one complete revolution, thus bringing the starting point once again opposite the key clavier. A perfect example of the street tableau may be seen in the film, "Dreigroschenoper" (Three Penny Opera), in which verses relating the atrocities of Mackie Messer are sung to the accompaniment of a buikorgel, illustrated by pictures of a murder, a fire, and . . . the rape of a minor widow. Might this not be compared to a modern comic book? Let it be a consolation to those who are tortured by worries (not entirely unfounded) about the influence of comics on our modern youth, that the young people pictured in the illustration, together with many others, were able to rise above these lurid playlets and become dignified grandparents without suffering psychic damage. When the demand for louder and better sounding street organs by-passed even the potential of the buikorgel, and the instruments gradually expanded to such proportions that the abdomens of the carriers, which of course did not grow along with the organs, could no longer carry them, a peg came into use as a support during the time the music was actually being played. Thus originated the so-called "pootorgel" (peg organ), which differed from

The *buikorgel* was often used in the 19th century to accompany dramatic songs illustrated by scenes painted on a poster. The audiences of such "films with music", even to those under fourteen years of age, needed nerves of steel.

The wording on the poster itself: "Terrible murder committed in Noord-Brabant on five persons, April 1843.

the buikorgel only by its larger size. When finally the point was reached where the instruments were mounted on three-wheeled carts to make possible ever-larger versions which were still easily moved, the wheeled street-organ was born.

It is interesting to note that the design of the organ cart has always remained the same, a low type of hand cart with large wheels right and left at the mid point, and one small one in the center front. Under the end at the rear it is necessary to have a short leg to prevent tipping while the organ is being played.

When the wheeled street organ had once come into being, it did not take long for the organs to become larger still, accompanied by a certain degree of modification in the structure. Although the buik and pootorgels were of the same height both in the front and the back, this was usually no longer the case with the new wheeled cylinder organs, where the front of the organ case was ordinarily built higher than the back. To clarify this point, we show here a side view of this type of case.

The sketch includes a circle, which indicates where the cylinder would be. The pipes of all types of organs had traditionally been placed in front of the cylinder for the sake of efficiency (compare the Floten-Uhr, serinette, buikorgel, and pootorgel). As these pipes became taller and more numerous, they had stuck out above the cylinder more and more. To accommodate them the organ case had to be built higher in the front. Added height was not necessary in the rear because no pipes could be installed above the cylinder and there was no other use that could

be made of this space. But this brings us up to the second
half of the 19th century and we have neglected many significant events in the development of the organ industry.

*Scene from the film "Three Penny Opera". The fire which Mackie Messer set
in Soho is being portrayed with the help of illustration No. 5, and for the
fifth time the buikorgel plays the melody which is now world famous.*

Let us return to Mirecourt, about 1800, to find out how
the modestly sprouting organ industry grew there and
spread elsewhere, particularly to the setting of Waldkirch.

The best-known organ factory at Mirecourt was that of the Poirot brothers. It was founded about 1780 by Nicolas Poirot and continued by his descendants until 1954 when the last representative of the family, Georges Poirot, died. We must also mention the firm Remy and Grobert, who, like Poirot, took up organ building during the 19th century, and whose instruments were particularly striking for their beautiful trumpets with their bells gracefully bent forward. As we shall see in chapter 7, they built mostly for fairs rather than for street use.

During the earlier time when these and other organ manufacturers were producing only small serinettes and portatives, about 1800, a bricklayer from the Black Forest, Ignaz Bruder, born in 1780, settled in Mirecourt. Ignaz, who had previously learned bricklaying in the Simon Forest but who had also been acquainted with the building of Floten-Uhren, now became acquainted with the French organ industry also.

Through this twofold knowledge of the organ trade, and because of his own inborn capabilities and musical sense, Ignaz was more or less predestined to become a capable organ builder. He took the money he had made as a bricklayer to buy a portative in order to study it and returned to the Simon Forest (Simonswald), where he succeeded in founding his own business in 1806. The currently popular Floten-Uhr and the completely new buikorgel were then being manufactured in this area. This business, which inclined more and more to buikorgels and later on, to the larger cylinder organs, grew constantly, due to the study which Ignaz Bruder made at that time of the art of organ building. When his firm moved to the industrial town of Waldkirch in 1843, Bruder became the founder of the Waldkirch organ industry, which became so well known

Street musicians of 1886 with a cylinder organ. If we did not know better, we would think it was Paul Verlaine in his latter days, accompanying his own song 'Ecoutez la Chanson Bien Douce' (Listen to the Sweet Song).

that the town has a folksong which the citizens sing with justifiable pride:

> In market places far and wide
> The organs sing their song:
> Listen, sing, and laugh with me . . .
> To Waldkirch I belong.

The barrel organ industry flourished in other places also about the middle of the 19th century. It is strange that organ-builders from Italy settled in France, Belgium, and Germany. Thus originated the firms of Frati in Berlin, Gavioli and Gasparini in France, and Pirolli and Fassano in Belgium. Thus, the Italian organ builders followed the example of the Italian street musicians, who also left their fatherland and roamed western Europe with their pianos and organs. We shall discuss the organ factories which flourished around 1900 and after more in depth in the second part of this book. Now we wish only to note that cylinder street organs were also built by the famous Viennese builder, Ferdinand Molzer (1855-1929), and in the city of Krazau in North Bohemia, where Riemer Bros. were the best-known builders.

In England, barrel organs were also built for church purposes. Evidently, capable organists could not always be found in the small town churches. The English firm of Flight and Robson built many hand-cranked barrel organs for churches, most of which have either been rebuilt into standard organs, or can be seen in museums. About the former barrel organ in the church at Gloucestershire a strange story is told. It is said that this organ continued to play at the end of the hymn so that the faithful had to repeat over and over, until finally indesperation they carried the instrument outside and placed it in the cemetery, where it continued to play after all the churchgoers had left. If this story is true, it could not have been a typical barrel organ. The music always dies away immediately when one stops cranking, for the bellows are not fed a new air-supply. Thus it would have been necessary only to . . . stop cranking! In two English churches these organs are still in use, not because a capable organist could not be found, but because the instruments have become famous curiosities. They are in the churches of Shelland in Suffolk and Barnston near Dunmow. In chapter 1 we stated that all aerophonic sound sources . . . thus all pipe organs . . . produce sound when air is blown into them. This blowing is almost always done by air, except in one most remarkable king of automatic pipe organ which was built during the second half of the 19th century in North America. We refer to the steam organ, sometimes called the "calliope", in which the pipes were blown by steam rather than air. By their very nature these instruments emitted a tremendous, piercing volume of sound. Think of an ordinary steam whistle on a ship! But this was exactly what was desired by Mr. J. D. Stoddard, who invented the steam organ in 1855 in Massachusetts. He wanted to use this instrument to call the believers to church! Helen and John Hoke tell us that the churchgoers preferred the regular bells and that Stoddard was forced to put his steam organ to a more worldly use. It is a fact that these "calliopes" were extensively used on the showboats that sailed the Mississippi. According to the Hokes, the number of passengers using the daily boat service on the Hudson River doubled after the introduction of steam organs on the boats. It is not known to us whether the calliope has sounded outside the U. S. excepting for the famous circus of Phineas Barnum, which took one along on a tour of Europe.

In this chapter on pipe organs, it is finally necessary to say something about one kind of instrument whose sound sources sometimes consist exclusively of various ranks of pipes, but sometimes also include strings, xylophones, and metallophones. You have it already; we are referring to the orchestrions. The history of the orchestrion starts around

1800 when the attempt began to imitate all the instruments of an orchestra and to bring them all together in one big instrument. In the next chapter we shall see how this effort resulted in the birth of an entirely new kind of mechanical musical instrument, one with freely vibrating tongues, and how the pioneers of orchestrion building, the Maelzel brothers and the Kaufmann family, did real pioneer work in the developing of these tongue (reed) instruments. Moreover, we shall see why the attempt to make "real" orchestra wind instruments play automatically failed. It did turn out to be possible to imitate the sound of these wind instruments quite faithfully. Reed instruments and pipe organs lent themselves much more readily to this attempt. The orchestrion builders specialized in building as many ranks of pipes into their instruments as possible, each with its own sound characteristics. In this way, organs with a wealth of different registers originated in the development of mechanical musical instruments. Through the building of these 19th century orchestrions, the foundation was laid for the refinement of registration which was to be stressed in the building of street, fair, and dance organs in the 20th century.

The term "orchestrion" we probably owe to Friedrich Theodor Kaufmann. After he and his father Friedrich had built their "Chordaulodion" and "Symphonion", he finished his chef d'oeuvre in 1851, christened the "Orchestrion" to distinguish it from all former Kaufmann family instruments. Other well-known orchestrion builders in the second half of the 19th century were J. H. Heller and Mermod Bros. in Switzerland and Jacob and Johann Blessing in Prague. Throughout all this, we must not forget that a very well-known instrument was built by a Dutchman which should be classed with the orchestrions. The brilliant Amsterdammer Diederick Nicolaus Winkel built his "Componium" as early as 1821. The specialty of this cylinder instrument with different ranks of pipes and percussion was that it could also improvise. Different themes of 80 measures each could be varied endlessly. Winkel built the instrument with the purpose of avenging himself on Johann Nepomuk Maelzel by eclipsing the latter's machines. Winkel had come into contact with Maelzel when the latter was demonstrating his "Panharmonikon" in Amsterdam in 1815. Maelzel, who wanted to imitate complete orchestras with his Panharmonikon and other instruments, was also looking for a way to create an automaton conductor, not because his Panharmonikon could not play without one, but because in the world of music there was a real need of an instrument which could indicate desired tempi accurately. When Maelzel discussed this problem with Winkel, the latter worked out the solution and entrusted it to Maelzel. This was how the metronome came into existence. Maelzel, however, abused Winkel's trust by claiming he had invented it himself. Unfortunately, the Componium did not bring Winkel any luck either. However ingenious the instrument was, financially it was a debacle for him. The machine is now in the instrument museum of the conservatory in Brussels. We feel that it really belongs in the Dutch museum, "Van speeldoos tot pierement" (From Music Box to Street Organ). Some 19th century orchestrion builders such as Bruder wanted their public not only to hear but also to see that their instruments imitated whole orchestras, and built in automaton musicians. Such an orchestrion is still in existence in the hotel "Zur Sonne" at Bleibach near Waldkirch. Behind a glass plate one sees a military band whose musicians play different wind and string instruments while a conductor beats time.

Nothing ever came of the goal of the early orchestrion builders to create instruments of the highest possible perfection which would be capable of performing classical music with true artistry. By the time the 20th century arrived with its technical improvements which would have made such a goal attainable, principally the use of paper

64

rolls and tracker bars instead of the earlier cylinders, the emphasis in mechanical music had changed. (The new type of orchestrion was patterned after pianolas and electrical pianos in their use of paper rolls.) Orchestrions by now had been popularized into mere cafe coin instruments which could be considered a cross between an electric piano and a dance organ, and a complete symphony orchestra was no longer the goal, but rather a modest dance orchestra.

We shall come back later to the further evolution of the mechanical pipe organ industry in part II. Now we must break off our study of the pipe organ for the sake of historical coherence with the other instruments being discussed in this section. We find we have to do this particularly because little is to be said about the development of the other instruments after the beginning of the 20th century. It will be possible to end our study of them at the same point in history when the real blossoming out of the barrel organ is just beginning; indeed, when the pierement (large book-type street organs) is just being born. The almost instantaneous collapse of the market for all the other automatic musical instruments coincides exactly with the rapid development of music reproducing machines (the phonograph) at the beginning of the 20th century which so quickly made the former old-fashioned and obsolete.

This switch from self-playing instruments to machines which only reproduced music concerned, in the beginning of the 20th century, only those instruments designed for the home. Therefore, the first ones to suffer were the reed organs, the string instruments, and the music boxes, while those instruments which were designed to be used in the open air or in big halls such as the street, fair, and dance organs could continue to develop without interruption.

Reed Organs 4

Like the pipe organ industry, that of the other mechanical musical instruments came to a real peak in the 19th century. This applies particularly to the reed organ and the music box, which will be discussed in chapter six. Although a penetrating historical explanation of this fact can be given only after a much more thorough investigation than has so far been carried out, we still must state that this happy development is largely due to the pioneer F. M. D. J. Engramelle and the stimulating influence of his work published in Paris in 1775, "La Tonotechnie, ou l'art de noter les cylindres et tout ce qui est susceptible de notage dans les instruments de concert mecanique". (Tonotechnique, or the art of pinning cylinders, and a complete study of music notation for mechanical musical instruments.) In this work you can read a comprehensive description of the method recommended by Engramelle for arranging music on cylinders with the required accuracy. He points out the great musicological significance of automatic instruments . . . provided the music is pinned on the cylinders with mathematical accuracy. The warnings he sounded and also his positive advice are so applicable even in our time that we feel we must quote him here. After having found that in many cases if no capable musician is available a perfectly-playing automatic instrument can be a boon, Engramelle admonishes composers that they must not be reluctant to arrange music for such machines because the art has always been shrouded in mystery. He further expresses his regret that this misapprehension has robbed the public of a treasure trove of creations from which it could have benefitted so greatly; that "music made to lift the soul and inspire harmonious feelings" has suffered irreparable losses; that many works of great composers could have been played and preserved which have now been lost; and that these composers could have directed the recording of their compositions according to their own wishes in the matters of time, interpretation, and expression, if only they had understood the art of arranging for automatic instruments.

The method proposed by Engramelle for arranging the music pattern on the cylinders is based on the premise that the division into measures, and hence, the rhythm, can be accurately established in a hand-cranked instrument by determining the number of times the handle must be turned to achieve one complete revolution of the cylinder, and that one can indicate the places where the pins have to be stuck into the cylinders most accurately with the keys of the clavier itself. Let us assume that 32 fast waltz measures can be arranged on the circumference of a canary organ cylinder, and that the handle will have to be cranked 48 times to accomplish one complete revolution. This means that for each beat of the 3/4 measure, the handle has to be turned half a turn. Now we wish to pin the following motif:

One starts by pushing in the g-key so that the metal point at the end makes a small mark in the wood of the cylinder. Then one turns the handle 3/4 turn farther, pushes in the a-key, and turns 1/4 turn again for the b-key. For the first beat of the next measure the handle has to be turned 1/2 turn. When the notes have been indicated on the cylinder in this way, the pins can be driven into the notches.

The system may seem so simple that it may be compared to the egg of Columbus, but it is a fact that the very painstaking work of drilling and pinning the cylinders in the correct places could never have been done with the required perfection if no advantage had been taken of this technique described by Engramelle.

To get to the real subject of this chapter, reed organs, we must first say something about the kind of music these instruments produce. The sound sources in this case are rectangularly-shaped tongues of a thin, springy material which fit exactly in openings of a metal plate, to which they are fastened. Because they are fastened at only one end, they can vibrate freely in the openings. In so doing, the free end moves slightly outside the surface of the metal plate. As we saw in chapter one, the reeds belong to the family of sound sources which are made to vibrate by blowing, so in this respect the idiophonic tongues resemble all aerophonic sound sources. As with all rectangularly-shaped sound sources, the vibration is faster and the tone higher the shorter the reed is. To clarify the foregoing, we present here a sketch of four reeds with the tones becoming higher from left to right. The rectangular figures indicate the tongues as well as the openings into which they fit. The circles indicate the rivets fastening the reeds to the plate.

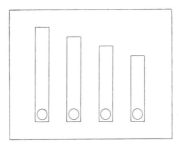

As with pipes, varying timbres and registers are possible with reeds. We mention in particular the difference between the reeds of an accordion and a harmonium. In the former, the plate to which they are fastened is as thin as they are; in the latter, it is much thicker. But on to the history of the reeds. When did harmoniums and accordions come into being? When were they made automatically playable? Or, were reeds possibly used first in automatically playing musical instruments? Alas, we will have to owe you the answers to these questions. There is not enough documented information on the subject. However, it is not impossible that reeds were invented by builders of mechanical musical instruments and that they were applied for the first time in this field. About 1800 there existed only three main groups of self-playing instruments, the carillons, pipe organs, and string instruments, but there was room for more! The builders were constantly striving to add other instruments to the roster. However, tremendous technical difficulties were encountered in connection with those instruments which could not be made to play automatically by the simple means of a clavier. (See chapter 1, page 21.) This was true especially of the brass wind instruments. The tones which are produced from these instruments are dependent on the way in which air is introduced into the mouthpiece by the musician. When it appeared impossible, therefore, to invent a machine which could play a real instrument, the attempt began to try to imitate the sound. This attempt was finally successful when reeds were built with a trumpet-shaped bell attached. But did these instruments exist before ordinary reed instruments were built? This question must be cleared up by more exhaustive musicological research. It is interesting, in any event, that the use of reeds in building ordinary instruments was propagated by builders of automatic ones, primarily. In this connection Buchner mentions the Maelzel brothers, the Kaufmann family, and Peter Heinrich. It is also noteworthy that the brothers Johan Nepomuk Maelzel (1772-1838) and Leonhard Maelzel (1783-1855), Johann Gottfried Kaufmann (1752-1818), his son Friedrich (1785-1866), and later also Friedrich's son, Friedrich Theodor Kaufmann (1823-1872) were famous builders of mechanical musical instruments, their goal being to imitate a complete symphony orchestra as faithfully as possible. Thus they became the founders of the orchestrion industry. Because they strove to enlarge the sound spectrum of their instruments constantly, they made extensive use of all kinds of reed registers to imitate wind and string instruments. You can still read the names of the instruments thus imitated on the stops of the larger harmoniums.

One of the oldest of these instruments using reeds in imitation of an orchestra was the "Panharmonikon" by J. N. Maelzel, exhibited in Paris as early as 1805. Buchner writes: "The Panharmonikon imitated not only wind instruments but also strings, in all dynamic variations." A short time later the Maelzel brothers built a second Panharmonikon which, according to Buchner, "surpassed the previous one in perfection." [1] About this second Panharmonikon, J. W. Enschede wrote in "Amstelodamum" (8th year, 1921) that it was shown by J. N. Maelzel in Amsterdam in or about 1812 and that it was activated like the Floten-Uhren, by a clockwork mechanism with cylinders and bellows. It also had percussion, and the sound was not produced by pipes, but by freely floating reeds. Enschede also wrote about this instrument: "It may be of historical interest to point out that this instrument, in its application of the reed, was the forerunner of the harmonium, the vocalion, and the American organ presently in vogue." No less a personage than Ludwig van Beethoven himself wrote a composition, titled "The Battle of Victoria", for this Panharmonikon.

Johann Gottfried Kaufmann also built, in 1805, an instrument with reeds which was christened the "Belloneon". It possessed twenty-four reeds with pipes in the shape of trumpets attached, and two cymbals. Similar instruments built later on were the "Salpingion" (Friedrich Kaufmann) which played the Hallelujah chorus by Handel among others, and also the instrument dating from the first half of

---

1. Page 79.

the 19th century with 24 reeds, also with trumpet pipes attached, built by Augustin Wolf. This instrument is preserved in the music department of the national museum in Prague.

This interest in imitating the sound of trumpets by means of reeds was manifested even more dramatically in the "trumpeters" built by F. Kaufmann, L. Maelzel, and P. Heinrich. These were large dolls which held to their lips a trumpet, which they appeared to blow. In reality, the sound was produced by reeds inside the head of the automaton, controlled by a cylinder mechanism built into the torso. These mechanisms were patterned after the Floten-Uhr, with a clockworks and a weight. F. Kaufmann's trumpeter, dressed in old Spanish costume, still shines in all its glory in the German museum at Munich. The one built by P. Heinrich (1817) was in the form of a lifesize horseback rider and played ten fanfares. Just how faithfully these reed devices imitated true trumpet tone may be indicated from two anecdotes recorded by Buchner, the first one concerning the Belloneon of J. G. and F. Kaufmann. Napoleon, who had retreated to the castle of Charlottenburg after the battle of Jena, was wakened during the night by the sound of trumpets sounding Prussian cavalry calls. He had the alarm sounded immediately because he thought they were being attacked by the enemy, but it was soon discovered that one of his comrades had come upon the Belloneon, built by Kaufmann for the king of Prussia, in the marble hall of the castle, and by accident had turned it on! The second anecdote concerns Leonhard Maelzel. His home was being besieged by revolutionaries in 1848, and he had his trumpeter, dressed in the uniform of a curassier, blow fanfares from an open window. The revolutionaries were thunderstruck. They thought a whole squadron of curassiers was stationed in Maelzel's house and fled.

During the middle of the 19th century, more and more reed instruments were made which were not provided with trumpet-shaped pipes. Until 1861 these instruments were furnished with the traditional cylinders and key claviers. Sometimes they were designed for use by street musicians like the "buik" (belly) organs, as was the case with the barrel reed organs made by Gavioli. To distinguish the real "buik" organs, which Gavioli gave the name "Harmoni-

A predecessor of our T.V.: monkeys playing musical instruments and performing magical tricks on the stage of a barrel reed organ.

pan", from his reed organs, he put the latter out under the name "Meloton". To compensate for the loss of the pan flutes (piccolo) with their graceful acorn-shaped finials, which had provided decoration for the front of the pipe organs, the Meloton organs were designed with a glass window in the front, through which one could observe the operation of the mechanism.

The majority of the reed organs was designed for use in the home. You may wonder, under what circumstances? This question gives us the opportunity to point out an interesting development. Looking back on the history of mechanical musical instruments which were to be used indoors rather than on the street, we see that in the course of four centuries they had become increasingly popular and thus had gradually gained ground. In the 16th and 17th centuries, virtually only royalty could enjoy the rare and costly objets d'art into which the small barrel organs were built. Sometimes monarchs had these curiosities commissioned for themselves, sometimes they gave them as gifts to kings of "friendly nations". We think here specifically of the creations of the Augsburg artists discussed in chapter 3. When, in the course of the 18th century, automatically-playing instruments were built not only in expensive custom cases, but certain types became more or less standardized, like the Floten-Uhren and the commode organs, then they spread beyond royal circles to the homes of the nobility and the wealthy in general. Through the beginning of the 19th century, however, mechanical instruments for the home remained so aristocratic and dignified that they still remained something for the wealthy. Excepting for canary organs, automatic instruments at that time were too costly to find a home outside the more wealthy circles in any event.

All this changed, however, when the reed-organ industry developed during the second half of the 19th century. They were much less expensive than the pipe organs which had been built into the Floten-Uhren and the commodes. Manufacturing reeds was much simpler and less time-consuming than building and voicing organ pipes. What had formerly been, of necessity, a handcraft, now lent itself to machine work and mass production. It was sufficient to build medium-sized instruments because reeds took much less room than pipes, and the cases were executed in simpler form. Because of all these factors, reed organs were within the reach of any individual at all who wished to own a chamber instrument with which music could be made automatically. Thus, reed organs of that era occupied approximately the same position which record players do in our own.

The popularization of automatic music which took place about a century ago had another important effect . . . there was an ever-increasing demand for an extensive repertoire. As long as an instrument is more or less a curiosity, it is accepted with a limited program of music, but as soon as it becomes common, the standards for both the instrument and its music become more exacting. If you had the (almost inconceivable!) good fortune to find a "buik" organ somewhere, you would not mind at all if it could play only eight tunes, and those very short, but if you could play only eight records of, at the most, one minute's playing time each, on your record player, you would not be much interested in it!

There was an urgent need to break through the twofold limitation of the repertoire. Twofold, because each melody was bound to the circumference of the cylinder (even with large barrel organs, no more than 64 fast waltz-measures could be performed), and because on one cylinder there was space for only eight (sometimes fewer, sometimes nine or ten, but never more than 12) different tunes to be pinned next to each other. While on this subject, let us note that the note barrel of the carillon is different from all the other variations which derived from it, for in the carillon the tunes are pinned right after each other. Immediately next to the pins controlling one key are those for the key beside it. In order to change the tune or tunes played, it is necessary to re-pin the barrel. In all other cylinder instruments, different melodies are pinned next to each other on the circumference of the cylinder. While the pins of one melody are activating the clavier, those of the other melodies are passing by without touching the keys. To make this physically possible, the keys have to be spaced a certain distance from each other, and their steel tips, as well as the pins and bridges on the barrel, have to be as thin as feasible so they will not take up too much space and there will be adequate clearance for the passing by of the pins and bridges which belong to the other tunes. Whenever a different melody is to be played, the cylinder is moved over by means of a special apparatus a very short distance. In the music box this happens automatically, but in all other instruments one has to manipulate the handle which is attached to the shifting device, an extension of the axle of the cylinder. The handle serves to lift the whole clavier temporarily so that the keys cannot be touched by the pins and bridges while the tune is being changed. This arrangement prevents any damage to either the pinning or the keys while the barrel is being moved. At this point the cylinder is free and can be moved laterally the desired number of notches to the new melody. The moral of the story is that an uninitiated person should never be allowed to attempt to operate the tune-changing apparatus of a cylinder instrument.

One way to extend the repertoire would be to buy several cylinders with the instrument. In the later years of the music box industry (1880-1900) this did come about. However, there are disadvantages. Think of the relatively heavy weight of the cylinders and the enormous size which

Reed organ with zinc discs.

a "cylindrotheque" (in contrast to a discotheque) would have. The problem was radically solved, however, when in 1861 another system was originated which was applied to reed organs; the system of claviers with keys which spring upward and which feel along for the punched pattern in cardboard discs or books. In 1861 the first reed organ, called the "Kartonium", to apply this new principle was built by J. A. Teste at Nantes. This is not to say that he invented the system himself. It is rather assumed that he combined the inventions of others and was the first to apply them in the manufacture of instruments which were turned out in any quantity. The Kartonium of Teste was remarkably similar to the later book organ of Gavioli. More about this in chapter 7.

Concerning music patterns in perforated cardboard, we must first turn our attention to the patent given to A. F. Seytre in 1842 at Lyon for the building of a music instrument in which "all kinds of melodies were produced by perforated cardboard with square or rectangular openings, depending on the notes to be played." However, more than a century earlier another invention was developed in the same city, from which Seytre surely must have derived his. In 1712 Joseph Jacquard invented the automatic weaving loom which functioned in a similar manner. Henri Bank describes Jacquard's invention as follows: "He mechanized the hand loom by punching the patterns of the fabrics in cardboard plates and having a special set of needles or keys feel along these plates with the result that the shuttles were propelled completely automatically through the frames, which were also automatic." [1]

Presumably Teste developed his system not only from Jacquard and Seytre, but also from others of his fellow countrymen who were working on automatically playing pianos. We must admit, however, that the dates we have been able to find in this research do not give a conclusive picture of the chronological order of all these inventions. According to Chapuis, a certain A. Zyob had built a book piano in 1842, the same year in which the patent was granted Seytre, based on the invention of Jacquard and called the "Autophone". This instrument was supposedly perfected in 1863 by Fourneaux.[2] Buchner, on the contrary, mentions neither Zyob nor Fourneaux, but draws attention to the "Antiphonel",[3] invented in 1846 by A. F.

---

1. "The Pierement", November 1956.
2. Page 129.
3. Page 25.

Debain. This was a mechanism which could be attached to any instrument with a normal piano clavier. At the top of the Antiphonel a much smaller clavier was constructed with narrow keys, set close together, which corresponded with the keys of the normal clavier. This upper clavier of the Antiphonel was played by a planchette (small board) on which the music pattern was laid out in protruding pins. Buchner goes on to say that in 1852 M. de Corteuil was granted a patent on a system which replaced the planchette with a perforated roll. If this is true, however, it would have to indicate that the player mechanism had been drastically changed as well, for the raised music pattern of the planchette depressed the keys to be played, but the perforated strip had to keep all the keys not being played depressed, so that those required in the music could spring up through the punched holes. In any case, it is certain that since 1843 French inventors have worked at the development of a book system which, as far as we can see, had a practical application for the first time in the Kartonium of Teste in 1861.

There is a Kartonium in the Brussels conservatory, according to Buchner, the only one extant. It is about the size of a small harmonium and the air is supplied the same way, with two pedals which must be pumped alternately by the player. At the top of the instrument is the key clavier we have just examined, strongly reminiscent of the clavier of our street organs. The music is in the form of perforated cardboard books which were "mangled" through the mechanism by two rubber rollers. This mechanism differed from that of the street organs in that there was no hinge provided for the upper section of the clavier. Therefore, when once a piece of music had been inserted, it had to be played through to the bitter end. We have devoted so much space to the Kartonium because it must be considered a forerunner of our book organs, to which we devote the entire second half of this book. As far as its mechanism was concerned, the Kartonium was a budding book organ. The principle difference between the Kartonium and the book organ is that the former did not function pneumatically as is the case with the other instrument.

That is the story of how the big leap forward from the cylinder system to the book system came about. It is surprising that after the birth of the Kartonium, the accent in the reed organ industry shifted completely to instruments which, although they were based on the principle of the Kartonium, in that they incorporated claviers with keys pressing upwards to "feel" the music pattern, played round perforated records and thus differed in this important respect from their predecessor. In a sense, one could consider this a step backwards compared with the use of paper rolls or books, because the length of the tune is limited to the circumference of a disc or cylinder, but in the case of rolls or books it depends solely on the arranger's desires and the melody itself.

The disc organs which were produced in great numbers toward the end of the 19th century may be divided into two groups, those with cardboard discs and those with ring-shaped zinc records. Well-known makes of disc organs were the "Intona", the "Ariston", and the "Manopan". In disc organs the clavier was always placed horizontally on the top of the case, and so the discs turned horizontally over the top of the instrument. One interesting variation of the reed organ was marketed under the "Kalliston" name. This instrument had the clavier arranged vertically on one side and was played by zinc bands which turned as rings around the ends of the case. On the top were a small drum and a set of bells which added rhythmic accent to the music of the reeds.

In all the disc and ring organs patterned after Teste, the keys of the clavier were directly and mechanically connected to the valves which controlled the flow of air through the reeds. When these keys were depressed by the music pattern, the valves closed. As soon as a key sprang up through a perforation in the record, the corresponding valve opened instantly and the flow of air caused the reed tongue to vibrate. This air supply was regulated by two bellows and a reservoir; the bellows were worked in the usual way by pump rods attached to the crankshaft.

The pneumatically operating reed organs with tracker bars and paper rolls which originated near the end of the 19th century were the zenith of the development of the genre. Those marketed by the Welte brothers under the trade name "Mignon" functioned extremely well technically and produced fine, beautiful music. We may safely state that of all the reed organs which hit the market about the turn of the century, the "Mignon" was definitely the most desirable! Nevertheless, so few of them have survived that today they would be called rare.

Mignon organ, reed instrument with paper rolls.

Thus we have seen that almost all the combinations of mechanisms discussed in chapter 1 were applied to reed organs during the second half of the 19th century. There are only two exceptions which have to be noted; electrical claviers and discs with burrs or projections on them. Of course, the electrical clavier goes without saying, since they were first applied in 1941, a few decades after the reed organ industry was ruined by the phonograph.

Strange to say, it never occurred in the reed organ industry that one system superceded another. On the contrary, until the entire industry perished completely with the rise of the phonograph and the radio, all the systems we have discussed existed side by side, even to the old cylinders. In this latter type the instruments with a small stage on top were especially attractive. While the music played, one could watch all kinds of spectacles behind the glass, such as the captivating monkeys in the illustration which performed magic tricks, played violin and cello and moved their heads and feet, all in time to the music. Could we not call such an instrument a forerunner of our modern T. V., which also combines pleasure for the eye and the ear?

At the end of the 19th century harmoniums were still being built in France, namely by Busson in Paris, which could be played from an ordinary keyboard or by a cylinder and a separate key clavier.

With the exception of trumpet instruments by Maelzel, Kaufmann and others, which were powered by springs (like music boxes) or weights (like Floten-Uhren), all reed organs discussed so far were cranked by hand. This does not apply, however, to two kinds of instrument which we want to mention in conclusion. First we must consider automatically playing accordions. Even though the player of this instrument had to regulate the air supply himself in the usual fashion; i.e. by extending and contracting the bellows, the accordion played automatically because in the right hand section was concealed a cylinder mechanism or a pneumatic system with rolls. The other of the two is the last instrument worth mentioning in the family tree of the reed organs, and one we may consider a counterpart of the pianola. It is a harmonium which can be played manually and automatically as well, with a tracker bar and paper rolls. As in some pianolas, the performer can regulate the tempo and dynamics with levers, following indications in dotted lines on the rolls. Such an instrument we could christen "Harmoniola".

The conclusion we must draw from this chapter is that reed organs occupy a most significant place in the history of automatically-playing musical instruments; because it was here that the development took place which would prove so important for all the other branches; namely, the advance from cylinders to books, discs, and rolls. Is it not remarkable that a similar development repeated itself later in the history of mechanical music reproduction? For, here also from the cylinder instruments (wax records) sprang the disc instruments (record players) and the instruments with rolls (tape recorders).

String Instruments 5

From the works of the 17th century music-theorists De Fluctibus and Kircher, we are led to believe that the history of automatically-playing string instruments started with a most bizarre sort of invention, in which two frames moved through each other. One of them was disposed horizontally, with the strings strung upon it, while the other moved up and down in a vertical direction through the first. In the vertical frame were slats, the number corresponding to the number of strings in the one through which it moved, and both strings and slats were evenly distributed. On the sides of the slats were pins which formed a music pattern, so that when the vertical slat frame was moved downwards, the pins would pluck the strings, pushing them down slightly and then releasing them again.

You will be curious about the method used to move the vertical frame up and down gradually and in constant tempo. This was done in different ways in the two instruments described by De Fluctibus. The first of these he christened "instrumentum magnum". The horizontal frame of this one was triangular, the strings running parallel to the base. In the top were the short, high-pitched strings, and along the base ran the long, bass strings. The vertical frame, which was rectangular in contrast to the horizontal one, was moved through the latter, one of its sides passing through an aperture in the peak of the triangle and the other through one in the exact center of the triangle's base, and it was suspended by a cable from a pulley. This pulley was part of a mechanism with a fly wheel, and the frame slowly descended by its own weight.

The second instrument was better yet! The horizontal frame was in the shape of a harp, which was lying on the top of a round barrel filled with water. On the water was a float the same size as the inner diameter of the barrel, with the vertical frame attached to it at a 90° angle. When the music was started the barrel was completely filled and the float was thus so high that the lowest pins of the music pattern were above the harp strings. Then a plug was pulled out of a drain pipe and the water slowly flowed out of the barrel, the water level and consequently, the float lowering at a steady rate of speed and the music pattern on the descending frame thus plucking the harpstrings.

Most unusual instruments! But who has ever heard one play? We certainly haven't! There is, so far as we know, no proof that they ever existed. De Fluctibus claims that he tried his "instrumentum magnum" himself, but we wonder if it might not have been a case of just an experiment. From the descriptions Kircher gives us, it is not clear whether we have to do with instruments that actually existed, or only with the technical fantasies of the theorists who wanted to show us how it could be done. This question could be answered only with diligent research. For the time being, we shall have to stick to our conviction that the oldest automatically playing string instruments were the cylinder spinets, which were built around 1600 in Augsburg by Samuel Biderman (died 1622). M. Mersenne also credits the automatic spinets to the Germans. They were often built into beautifully decorated art cases, just as were the pipe organs manufactured in Augsburg during the 16th and 17th centuries. This is evident from the specimens which have been preserved in various museums (Breslau, Vienna, and Dresden). They were activated by spring mechanisms like those used later in music boxes. This went also for a unique instrument called the "Harfanette d'amour" now located in the music department of the national museum in Prague. The typical cylinder system in this instrument acts upon small hammers which strike the lower extremity of the strings, which are strung on a gracefully rising soundboard decorated with an angel's head at the top. There are also cherubs sitting on either side of the base of the soundboard.

The manufacture of automatically playing string instruments for the salon during the 18th and the beginning of the 19th centuries never developed to the extent that pipe organs did. The harp clock to be seen in the above-mentioned museum in Prague would have to be considered a great rarity, compared to the Floten-Uhren, which were turned out in great numbers at this same time. However, in the realm of street instruments, it was quite another story. Not only cylinder organs, but also cylinder pianos . . . in great numbers . . . were produced for the street musician trade. In fact, the two had so much in common that the pianos were sometimes mistakenly called "piano-organs". Of course, this is strictly a misnomer, for the music is not produced by pipes at all, but by strings. If there ever was such an instrument, it would have had to be the orchestrion, which actually does combine the two into one instrument. Street pianos were made primarily in Italy and Spain. Because the Italian piano grinders roamed other countries with their instruments, the Netherlands among them, street pianos became a familiar sight all through western Europe. I remember similar instruments playing along the boulevards in the Belgian beach resorts in 1929. Now they have disappeared practically everywhere except in Spain and Curacao, where they are still used as street instruments. The fact that these pianos still live on in the memories of many individuals as exciting, delightful sounding instruments is due partly to the various percussion effects and even glockenspiel music which augmented the basic piano in many instruments.

Two of the few remaining street pianos have found their way to the Netherlands in recent years in a quite remarkable way. One of them made its way here from England when the English town of Bath "adopted" Alkmaar in 1945. Money was collected for the occasion with the help of one of the barrel pianos still remaining in the country. Along with the money, the instrument itself was presented to the town of Alkmaar. The municipality now zealously watches over the instrument and it has been exhibited at various organ competitions by Alkmaar cheese carriers as a curiosity in recent years. A striking combination of two kinds of folklore from very different backgrounds! The other piano is now in the museum "From Music Box to Pierement" and was given to the institution by the Utrecht attorney, Mr. Rink, who has many precious memories of this instrument. As a small boy, he always ran after it, for it had stolen his heart . . . many of us have done the same thing! This piano, made in Italy, was played by the old Italian Randolfi in Tiel. When he had to give up playing in the streets, because of age, he presented it to the boy who had always loved it so much. If only all street musicians disposed of their instruments in such a wonderful way!

Most of the street pianos still in existence are most likely found in England. Canon Wintle is to thank for this fact, as was evident from a series of lectures he gave in 1954 for the B. B. C. He and other friends of the barrel piano have even roamed the streets at times with these antique instruments, disguised in the proper attire, of course, complete to false moustaches, etc. If you would like to see a barrel piano in its proper setting, do try to see the most original movie, "Robbers' Symphony", by Friedrich Feher. The catchy music of this film, composed by Feher himself, we have also arranged for various of the pierement. Since then, the music has conquered the hearts of many organ friends, just as the movie conquered the hearts of its audiences. In it you can see, among other things, that the shape of a street piano is exactly like that of the standard parlor instrument. The difference lies only in the fact that instead of the ordinary keyboard there is a huge barrel with a corresponding key clavier, and also that the side of the instrument's case which is generally unseen because it is against the wall in your

The street piano in the film "The Robbers' Symphony, which gradually became more of a woods-and-snow piano.

living room, has now become the front of the street piano and has been duly decorated in one way or another. Sometimes there are discs which revolve during the music, displaying various spectacles like the battle of Waterloo. Often the entire case is decorated all over with little mirrors.

This latter type of decoration was even more typical of another variety of piano, those used in cafes. They worked the same way their street cousins did, excepting that it was not necessary to stand and crank them. They were powered by a huge spring motor which had to be wound up with a crank by the customer. The appearance of the cafe piano was somewhat different too, in that it was built more like a large rectangular cupboard, decorated with numbers of mirrors, bunches of glass beads, and bronze statues. To complete the description and to be absolutely certain that you know which machines we are describing, we have only to mention that they were sometimes called . . . . most disrespectfully . . . . "Tingeltangels"! Let us forget this sobriquet immediately! A well-known builder of these cafe pianos was Pierre Paul van Roy of Aalst, now a septuagenarian. Sometimes all the strings were struck by hammers, but in some instruments only half of them were and the remainder were plucked. This plucking action could be kept up rapidly for held notes, as in the playing of the mandolin. Often idiophonic sound sources were added, such as metallophone or xylophone. These machines usually played only upon inserting money, to make them economically profitable. One of the cafe pianos of P. P. van Roy is now in the museum, "From Music Box to Pierement". Around the end of the 19th century, perforated books, discs, and rolls were used in automatic string instruments along with the original wooden barrels, just as they were all used at the same time in reed organs. The "Guitharmony", an instrument built by Gavioli in Paris, had a cylinder mechanism. It consisted of a guitar with a mechanism

The works of a cafe cylinder piano, with xylophone (left) and metallophone (right). What happens when it plays can be guessed from the quotation from Horatio which some wag fastened over it: "Dulce est desipere in loco", meaning "It is sweet to be foolish in this place."

attached for plucking the strings. According to one of their catalogues, Gavioli also made book pianos in the shape of an ordinary instrument, as well as the "piano-melodico", shaped like a cembalo, which plucked the strings rather than struck them. This was also the case in the automatic zithers, which were made in two styles; automatic and semi-automatic, the latter applying the system of a clavier with keys springing up through holes in paper rolls. This combination is very rarely encountered, for this type of clavier usually takes books or discs of a sturdier material than paper, which is too prone to being torn by the metal keys. The semi-automatic zither consisted of a real instrument upon which was mounted a mechanism for playing the melody (possibly two voices) automatically but not the accompaniment. The chords were indicated on the paper rolls by numbers, so that one could play the instrument by following them as they appeared without any knowledge of music. The fully automatic zither, or "Chordephone" as it was called, was played by discs with metal burrs or projections on them, just as in the disc music boxes made around 1900. (See chapter 6, page 99.) It must be established, however, that a disc-playing string instrument was the exception.

All the string instruments discussed so far have worked from key claviers. The zenith in the development of automatically-playing string instruments was achieved, however, only with the adaptation of the pneumatic principle. During the first decades of the 20th century were built the so-called pianolas, with tracker bars and paper rolls. Some of the well-known manufacturers were Aeolian (the "Duo-Art"), Hupfeld (the "Phonola"), and Pleyel (the "Pleyela"). One interesting refinement of the last two manufacturers was the provision of hand controls for regulation of the dynamics and tempo as indicated by inked lines on the rolls of music. The operator, therefore, had more or less the illusion of playing himself. Thus it is evident that the manufacturers strove to develop automatic playing systems capable of as nearly perfect a re-creation of the original performance as possible. The ultimate in perfection was achieved by the Welte Bros. of Freiberg, builders of the "Welte-Mignon" pianos, of which the special rolls were arranged beforehand by no less than the performing artist himself. The achievement of this extremely ingenious mechanism was the reproduction of the finest shadings of expression in the original performance. In a sense, one could say that this was already automatic music reproduction.

The commercial counterparts of these parlor player-pianos were the "electrical pianos" which could be found during the first decades of this century in cafes, inns, etc. They were pneumatic machines with tracker bar and paper roll, run by electric motor. The tempo and dynamics were constant, though, and could not be regulated by the customer. In our country they were imported and installed by the orchestrion factory Beckx-de la Fai in Tegelen, among others, which concern flourished until about 1930. The difference between these electric pianos and the orchestrions was that the former were purely string instruments, while orchestrions combined strings with registers of pipes and percussion too.

The instruments to come last in the evolution of the field of mechanical musical instruments were the automatically-playing violins. In chapter 1 we pointed out that there were tremendous technical difficulties to be solved in making these instruments self-playing. These were twofold. In the first place, some means had to be devised of bowing the strings. Secondly, a mechanism for fingering them had to be perfected. Actually, a solution to the first problem had already been long in use in the "hurdy-gurdy", which could be called a semi-automatic violin. The performer had to manipulate the strings in order to determine the pitch, but all he had to do to bow them was turn a crank, for the bowing was done by a rosined wheel inside, revolved when the crank was turned. The well-known singer, Rob van der Bas of Blaricum owns one of these instruments.

We read in Buchner [1] that the first completely automatic

---

1. Page 100.

violin was built in 1908 in the U. S. A., the "Virtuosa", bowed by rotating discs like the hurdy-gurdy and fingered by electromagnets pressing down small buttons on the strings. Much better-known were the violins of the Hupfeld firm in Leipzig, makers of the "Dea Violina", built with three violins located inside a rotating circular bow. Here also the fingering was done by a series of buttons, corresponding to the air ducts of a tracker bar with paper rolls.

In conclusion we must mention the "Violinista" invented in 1913 in France by Aubry and Boreau. This instrument consisted of a standard violin, played by an actual bow which moved to and fro automatically. Here, too, the fingering was done by a pneumatic mechanism controlled by a tracker bar and paper rolls. These violins were invented too late, however, to become a commercial success. Attention was by then already focussed too much on the new systems of sound reproduction.

Music Boxes 6

How often does it happen that music lovers who show, at the most, a certain condescending interest in automatic musical instruments, are suddenly touched by the subtle music of a music box and are moved, like Cecile Lauber, to proclaim aloud or muse to themselves, "The music box is the sweet melody of simple hearts." (La boite a musique est la douce melodies des coeurs simples.)

This natural moving quality of the music box because of its inherent simplicity is a perfectly logical consequence of the fact that this instrument is exclusively automatic, having been created in this form originally in contrast to carillons, organs, and string instruments, which can also be played by musicians. Is this not largely the solution to the enigma of why we are so completely cast under a spell by one automatic musical instrument and are not nearly so moved by another? An example may clarify this theory. When we hear carillon music it may put us immediately in a more cheerful frame of mind, but at the same time it takes a concert by a living carillonneur . . . preferably on a quiet summer night . . . to evoke a really emotional reaction. On the other hand, many of us brighten up immediately and are touched in a very special way by the music of a Carl Frei organ. But is this phenomenon due to the fact that this instrument, too, was born and developed as an automatically-playing instrument? When we think over this theory within the framework of the entire history of mechanical music, we think we can perceive a pattern which explains all this. The efforts of the builders of mechanical musical instruments have always been largely aimed at imitating or equalling, as far as possible, the music of human performers. This effort reached a zenith with the development of the pianolas, especially the Welte-Mignon, which was designed actually to reproduce the original performance. However, no matter what the technical perfection of the mechanism involved, performance by a human could not be surpassed, short of perhaps the execution of complicated chords at a fast tempo or some other trick of composition physically impossible for the human hand. In practice even this did not play a role because the music patterns made for the automatic instruments were the identical music literature composed for human musicians. (Excepting for the special compositions of Haydn, Mozart, and a few other composers discussed in chapter 3.) In some instances the efforts of the manufacturers were directed, how-

The cylinder music box in its most basic format. The least complicated of the mechanical musical instruments.

ever, towards the creation of entirely new instruments with a sound character of their own, not found in any of the instruments playable by musicians. It was in this way that automatic musical instruments with a very special, quite unique style of music came into being. We think in this regard particularly of the music box and the different kinds of street organ which we shall discuss in the second half of this book. Just as we are acquainted with those who love a particular kind of music (string orchestra, symphony orchestra, piano, carillon, etc.), so also are there those who are particularly attached to a certain type of music box or street organ. But . . . there is one important difference! A devotee of the carillon will always prefer hearing a carillonneur to a mechanical player, just as a lover of the piano will greatly prefer the living artist to the pianola, and one of the violin, a renowned virtuoso to one of Hupfeld's "Dea Violina" machines. However, when one is enamoured not of the carillon or the violin but street organs, the picture is not the same. One loves the street organ, period, although there is one parallel. Just as concert goers honor those who have performed the music by applauding, so lovers of music boxes and street organs feel they have to show their feelings of appreciation for their musical pleasure to those who have brought it about. This feeling does not bring them to the doors of soloists and conductors, but to the manufacturers and music arrangers.

But . . . to return to the music box. Is it not possible that Antoine Favre, the inventor of the system of vibrating thin steel teeth by way of a cylinder mechanism, these teeth thus becoming a sound source directly, himself felt intuitively something of what we wrote at the beginning of this chapter, when he showed his invention which he labelled "carillons sans timbre ni marteau" (carillons without bells or hammers) to the "Societe des arts" at Geneva in 1796? An interesting sidelight of this invention is that it was actually the study of an automatic musical instrument, the miniature carillon of the clockmaking industry, that led to the development of a wholly new automatic instrument which would gradually evolve into something infinitely nobler and finer than ever appeared possible with the original miniature carillons. For it was the use of these tiny carillons in watches that paved the way for the music box. Even at this greatly reduced size, the carillon was still of necessity a number of bells with a traditional cylinder mechanism. However one tried to save space by giving the bells a flat shape and nesting them inside each other, it was unavoidable that musical watches should be somewhat heavy and cumbersome. It must have been an effort at simplification which gave Favre the brilliant inspiration of replacing the balls and hammers with simple steel teeth plucked directly at the very tip by tiny pins in a revolving cylinder. Where previously the automation of an already existing instrument necessitated adding one or more mechanisms, now a completely new principle originated through an attempt at simplifying a too-complicated mechanism. As an outgrowth of the new watches with cylinder mechanisms playing on vibrating steel teeth, two further refinements resulted. In the first place, the added space gained by the elimination of the hammers and bells inspired an effort to do the same sort of thing with the cylinder. This was accomplished by replacing it with a disc studded with pins equally as fine as those in the cylinders around 1810. The steel teeth to be plucked by the pins were now mounted flat above the disc and the ends were shaped turned downwards just far enough to be engaged by the pins passing underneath. The second improvement was the building of these music devices for their own sake apart from timepieces. This happened only after Favre's invention had been considerably improved in three major areas between 1815-1820. For one thing, the steel teeth were made from one piece of steel, called a comb, instead of individually or in small groups. These teeth grew gradually shorter from one end to the other as they had to be tuned higher and higher. (Even in ordinary combs for the hair it is sometimes found that the teeth grow shorter from one end to the other, and a corresponding change in the sound produced by scraping one's thumbnail over their tips from one end of the comb to the other may be discerned.) The inventor of this "clavier d'µne seule masse" (one-piece comb) was Francois Lecoultre.

It is to the same Francois Lecoultre that we owe the sonorous bass notes which have become standard in music boxes. To achieve the dark, deep, satisfying tone of this register, lead weights were fastened to the underside of the longest teeth, making them vibrate much more slowly and thus lowering their tone several octaves. The refinement which we owe to Francois Nicole was also vital. He invented a method of preventing the contact of the pins with vibrating teeth. To this end he placed under the tips of the teeth

A disc music box: The Symphonion.

tiny dampers of springy material which made contact with the approaching pins and made possible a supple, pure vibration of the tooth and was indispensable for good sound quality.

As a result of this threefold improvement by Lecoultre and Nicole on the invention of Favre, a music box industry started up about 1820 which would prosper and enlarge at an ever-increasing rate even into the 20th century. The most important centers of this industry were Geneva and Sainte-Croix, which eventually exported music boxes all over the world, even to the Americas and Asia. Prague and Vienna also were centers of manufacture. Ever more beautiful models were produced of all varieties and combinations with many improvements of which we shall give a survey. The cylinder system was maintained throughout until up to the last ten years of the 19th century, when a a disc-playing mechanism was adapted to the combs. All boxes were powered by a spring mechanism, at first wound by a chain device and key, but later by a special handle.

The number of melodies which could be pinned on the circumference of a cylinder varied from four to twelve. The repertory usually consisted of selections from operas and operettas, and other popular tunes of the day, whose titles were listed on beautiful tune-cards inside the lid of the rectangular wooden box used to house the mechanism. These cases were usually of beautiful wood, sometimes with an inlay of mother-of-pearl. They were important not only from an aesthetic point of view and as storage space, but were also an indispensable part of the instrument, since they functioned as soundboards without which the sound of the combs would be thin and faint. Through the combination of music combs and wooden cases, the clear, warm sound we expect in a good music box is created. In the cylinder boxes a special attachment caused the automatic

Music box with zither, drums, castanets, and Chinese bell-strikers.

shifting of the cylinder a few centimeters after each melody to the next tune, and after playing the last one it jumped all the way back to the beginning position again. By moving a special lever provided for this purpose, this shifting could be cancelled and the machine would play the same tune repeatedly. A steady tempo was guaranteed by a fan mechanism. It is a pity that in many of the music boxes that have survived, the teeth of the combs are broken or the pins are so badly worn they barely touch the teeth, if at all, or the dampers under the tips of the teeth are broken or bent due to old age, causing an annoying rasping sound during the playing of the music. These defects are practically irreparable. Fortunately, this is not the case when troubles appear in the spring mechanism, the fan, etc.

Now that we have described the prototype of the cylinder music box, we shall describe the many interesting varieties and attachments added as music boxes were kept up-to-date and expanded during the second half of the 19th century:

The forte-piano music box, in which there were two combs, one to play the loud passages and one for the soft;

The mute, or harp attachment which could be lowered to rest on the combs and produced a tone quality not unlike a zither;

Music box with a marquis playing the violin.

The addition of bells, drums, and castanets which added a gay touch and accented the rhythm;

Animated dolls and other figures which provided a visual fascination;

The organ box, which had the clavier of a tiny reed organ between the combs of the music box and thus played the two types of music together;

A further refinement of the latter type, but with a tiny pipe organ like the serinet rather than reeds;

Music boxes on matching tables with drawers for storage of a "cylindrotheque".

Music boxes with automatically changing cylinders.

The musical movements were installed not only in the traditional inlaid cases, but in all sorts of novelties and objets d'art, greatly reduced in size, of course. They have been put into jewel boxes, Tyrolean chalets, picture albums, cigaret boxes, chairs, toilet paper holders, etc. There were even oil paintings with musical movement and a real clock dial in a tower sending forth carillon music, and lovely little landscapes under large glass domes with a musical movement playing while boats roll on an ocean, birds sing and fly, water runs in a tiny brook, and perhaps a marquis plays the violin.

Of course, it was increasingly necessary to enlarge the repertory of music boxes, just as it was in other types of drawing-room instruments. The fact that a readily-changeable disc mechanism was a long time in appearing was due to the technical difficulties which had to be overcome in such an instrument. It finally meant that an extra clavier had to be added, for the music comb is such that it readily lends itself to playing directly by cylinder with pins (The music comb was originally invented opposing such a cylinder), but cannot be played directly by discs. One of the reasons why the manufacturers clung to the cylinder, bulky

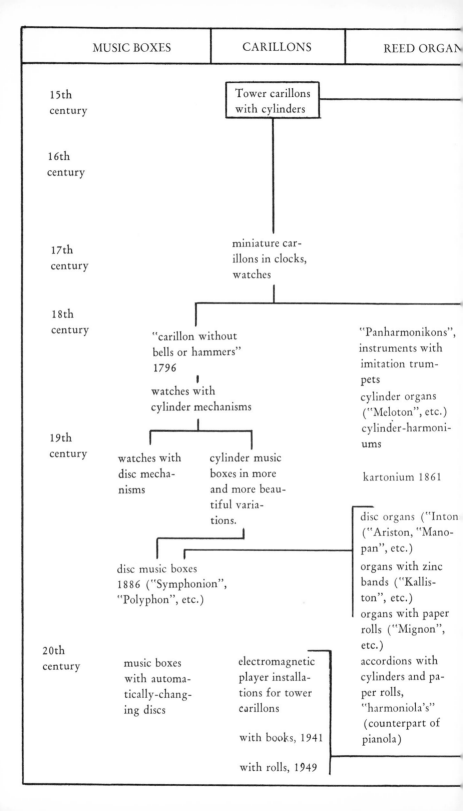

	MUSIC BOXES	CARILLONS	REED ORGAN

15th century — Tower carillons with cylinders

16th century

17th century — miniature carillons in clocks, watches

18th century

MUSIC BOXES: "carillon without bells or hammers" 1796 → watches with cylinder mechanisms

REED ORGAN: "Panharmonikons", instruments with imitation trumpets; cylinder organs ("Meloton", etc.); cylinder-harmoniums

19th century

MUSIC BOXES: watches with disc mechanisms; cylinder music boxes in more and more beautiful variations.

REED ORGAN: kartonium 1861

disc music boxes 1886 ("Symphonion", "Polyphon", etc.)

REED ORGAN: disc organs ("Inton ("Ariston, "Manopan", etc.); organs with zinc bands ("Kalliston", etc.); organs with paper rolls ("Mignon", etc.)

20th century

MUSIC BOXES: music boxes with automatically-changing discs

CARILLONS: electromagnetic player installations for tower carillons — with books, 1941 — with rolls, 1949

REED ORGAN: accordions with cylinders and paper rolls, "harmoniola's" (counterpart of pianola)

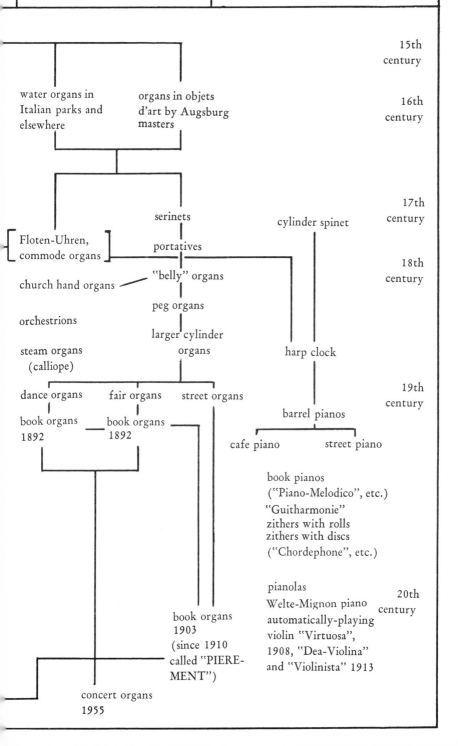

Music box with large, vertically-rotating discs.

and cumbersome as it was, for so many years, was that there seemed to be no immediate solution at hand.

When finally a disc mechanism was invented which could play music combs, it was done by placing an assembly of rotating gears, called "star-wheels", in front of the comb. When the disc, placed directly above this assembly, was set in motion by the spring motor, the small projections bent out from its surface made contact with one of the points of the star-wheel causing it to revolve part of a turn. At the same time, one of the other points of the moving star-wheel lifted the tip of one of the teeth in the comb and plucked it.

The disc music box was invented in Germany and put on the market for the first time in 1886 by O. P. Lochmann in Gohlis near Leipzig, and the machine was christened the "Symphonion". His patent on the disc system did not do him much good, because many others manufactured and marketed similar instruments during the last ten years of the 19th century. The best-known factory was that of Polyphon in Leipzig. One of its branches was the "Regina Music Box Co." in the United States. Although the disc boxes were built in all shapes and sizes (the smallest ones were sometimes put in picture albums), the best-known model is the large upright with a disc storage cabinet at the bottom and the revolving disc visible in the top section through a glass door. In many of the disc boxes two combs played simultaneously, in unison. Two different points of a star wheel plucked teeth of two different combs together. The two teeth sounding together were always tuned to the same note but with a slight variation of pitch, producing a characteristically rich, ringing tone.

The large cabinet music boxes were primarily used in cafes, usually playing, like the mirrored barrel pianos, only if a coin was inserted in the slot. The innkeeper could regulate the type of coin used if the coin-slot mechanism was of the tipping-scale variety by adjusting the tension of the spring on the scale. Otherwise he could enlarge the hole in the coin receptacle of the tripping mechanism, so that if too small a coin was used, it would fall through into the money drawer underneath and no music would be forthcoming, and the customer would not get his coin back, either! If the coin was big and heavy enough, the scales would tip and the disc would play normally. When the "Regina Music Box Co." invented an automatic disc changer for music boxes in 1896, the forerunner of the "juke-box" was born, the instrument which later would replace all the music boxes.

The Origin of the Pierement (Street Organs)

7

When these typically Dutch organs play in the streets of Amsterdam, one cannot help but feel, "These wonderful instruments must never be allowed to disappear!" This brings up two questions: is the pierement really Dutch, and is there any danger of its disappearance?

The first question we will consider in this chapter. Later on we will give a general outline of the history of the pierement from circa 1900 to the present, and finally we will try to answer the second question in the last chapter of this book.

First, let us define what we mean when we speak of "pierement". Referring to part one of this book, which distinguishes the various automatic musical instruments, we may define the pierement as automatic street pipe organs, the mechanism of which is activated by the turning of a wheel.

However, under this broad definition would fall both the old cylinder or barrel street organs and the so-called "book" street organs. Nowadays the word "pierement" refers only to the book street organs. The conception of the public at large of the pierement is far removed from the old barrel organs, both in outward appearance and in its music. It was not until the early part of this century that the book-organs appeared on the public streets and became well-known, not only to the knowledgeable in the world of organs, but also to the general public, which gave it the name "pierement". J. F. M. den Boer came to the conclusion after extensive research that this word originated

09

around 1912, long after the book organs first appeared.[1] Den Boer points out that before 1912, the word "pierement" never appeared in the papers, journals, or other literature having to do with organs. However, this word does appear in Querido's "De Jordaan", copyright 1912. Querido found it necessary to include the word "pierement" in a special list of words not known to the general reader. Let us note at this point that from the standpoint of systematic "pierementology", we must also distinguish the street organ from the other types of automatic organ, such as the fair organ and the dance-hall organ, which we shall analyze later. Thus, the pierement should be defined as an automatic pipe-organ, played on the street and operated by the turning of a wheel and the movement of a perforated, self-folding cardboard book acting upon a sort of tracker bar.

Before going deeper into the origin of the book-organ and the development of the pierement, we want to delve a little further into the origin of the word "pierement". However, here there are many opinions and educated guesses. A popular, but to me unsound theory is that the word pierement comes from "Pierre Ament," the name of an organ builder who is supposed to have lived in the city of Roermond. For example, we read in the journal St. Gregorius of July-August, 1947: "There once existed in Roermond a street organ factory. The owner, Pierre Ament, lettered his name at the bottom of a corner on the front of his organs." As far as is known to us, there is, however, no proof of the existence of this "Pierre Ament". For six years the "Kring van Draaiorgelvrienden" (Society of Friends of the Street Organ) has been diligently seeking out data on all street organ factories, builders, rental agencies, and

---

1. "Pierement, the Amsterdam Street Organ", published in "Amstelodamum", volume 18, 1951.

dealers, both domestic and foreign. The results of this inquiry have been very good, especially quantitatively. Nowhere, however, was there mentioned a "Pierre Ament", either in Roermond or anywhere else. We cannot conceive that of the more than 1100 members of this organization, not a single one would have come across this "Pierre Ament" if he really existed. If course, it is still not an utter impossibility. We ask the reader, therefore, to send us any information he might have concerning this person. If such information is forthcoming, we will mention it in the next printing of this book. Until such time, however, we shall have to agree with J. F. M. den Boer in his earlier mentioned article. He considers it probable that "pierement" comes from the old Dutch verb "pieren", which means "to enjoy by dancing in the round". The suffix "ement" is common in the Dutch language. An amusing pun, quoted by den Boer, is attributed to an organ player who complained he had a "mankement" (ailment) in his pierement.

But let us return to the consideration of the origin of the pierement as a musical instrument. This we owe to the combination of three historical events: the founding of a large street-organ rental agency in Amsterdam circa 1875 by the blind Leon Warnies of Belgium; the construction of the first book organs in 1892 by Anselme Gavioli in Paris, and the introduction of these book organs in the Netherlands as street organs, or pierement, by Warnies. We shall put these three events under the magnifying glass individually.

THE STREET ORGAN RENTAL AGENCY
OF WARNIES

In chapter three we described the development of the portable organs and the street cylinder organs during the nineteenth century. We noticed how Mirecourt and Wald-kirch became centers of this steadily expanding industry. At this point we should mention that these cylinder organs were not solely made for street musicians, but also for fairs and dance halls. The fairs in particular became important clients. In the dance halls, the cylinder organs took their place, figuratively speaking, next to the cylinder pianos, the orchestrions, and the music boxes. For a good understanding of the following, it is necessary to remember the difference between fair, dance, and street organs.

Street organs were in use in several west-European countries at the end of the nineteenth century, but, as far as is known to us, only in Amsterdam was any order created in the business through the founding, in 1875, of the rental agency of Leon Warnies. In Amsterdam the professional musician replaced the itinerant musician who travelled from town to town with his music box or cylinder organ. The professional musician rented his instrument from the agency of Warnies, who saw it as a personal honor to keep his instruments in top condition. Under these conditions, the street organ business reached a high level of proficiency and technical perfection in Amsterdam. We are convinced that this professional approach . . . next to the introduction of the book organs . . . was one of the main reasons for the positive development of the street organ in the Netherlands, as opposed to that in other countries.

Everywhere else the musical instruments used in the street have gone slowly downhill until nowadays it is extremely rare to see one outside of Holland, and then they are played by individuals one would term "relics from a dusty past". We shall return to this deterioration of street instruments later on.

112

Leon Warnies, who founded the first street organ rental agency in Amsterdam in 1875.

113

From Warnies' company one could rent the new wheeled cylinder organs as well as the older "belly" organs for the first few decades after 1875. It is interesting to note (before we plunge into the material on the book organs with the likely result that we shall become so absorbed in them we will pay no more attention to the old barrel organs) what happened to all these early organs. The story will be short and parts of it rather gloomy. Some of them were rebuilt to play the new books, but others fell into the hands of street musicians playing the fair circuits, unfortunately, and in general they did not take care of them. The result was that they played worse and worse, and at last had to be retired, after which they were lost to woodworm and moisture. This tragic development took place during a rather short time span, for as late as 1930 I used to see numerous travelling musicians with their organs reporting to the police station at 7:00 o'clock on the first Saturday of the May fair in Groningen. The chief of police, Molenaar (who came from a very artistic and musical family), gave the instruments an inspection, and it was extraordinary that even the most ghastly specimens were always granted permission to add musical embellishment to the city of Groningen for ten whole days. Could it have been pity on the part of the chief? Or was the inspection of the organs merely an excuse to look into the character and background of the musicians themselves? The result of these organ-orgies during the Mayfair was that the two officially licensed organ grinders in Groningen just had their instruments tuned, painted, and checked over because they could not even earn a crust of bread with so much competition. Now there are only a few barrel organs left in the Netherlands, and those purely by accident. One of them was still played until a few years ago in and around Wageningen, a unique case of one individual, old Mr. Haagsman, who remained faithful to his hand organ. Another was located by

114

one of the most active sleuths of the "Kring van Draaiorgelvrienden", M. J. L. M. van Dinteren at Geleen, who just
managed to rescue it from oblivion. Both of these veterans,
together with a third, now being restored by the organ
builder Louis van Deventer of Brummen, are destined for
the museum, "Van speeldos tot pierement". The fact that
all the other wheeled barrel organs were lost is, as we said
previously, primarily due to the lack of respect of those
who owned them. Not too long ago I found a cylinder organ in Limburg which had been largely consumed by
woodworms. What do you think of the mentality of the
owner who could tell me that the instrument was rare and
he would part with it for no less than $300.00 (f 1200),
but who on the other hand could not take the trouble to
take the organ to the garage and to store it in such a
way as to prevent any further decay? Without a doubt, this
decay is complete at the printing of this book.

Finally, you will want to know what happened to the
"belly" and peg organs rented out by Warnies. Some of
them were rented out for quite some time in Amsterdam
. . . even after the book organs were in general use, some
of the licensees still continued to prefer the smaller barrel
organs, which were much easier to move about and required
less labor. The Amsterdam police, who gave out annual
permits to organ grinders, came to the realization in 1924
that there were not enough of these smaller instruments
left to continue issuing the permits, and decided just to
let them die a natural death. The three holders of permits
who still were playing barrel organs in 1924 were allowed
to keep them. One of these was the well-known Ate Wie-
linga, nick-named "Half-Legs". One year later he, too, was
converted to the book organ. In 1930, the last barrel organ
finally disappeared from the streets. Since then there has
been nothing in Amsterdam to serve as a reminder of the

street music of the 19th century. The "belly" and peg organs were destined to meet the same fate as the wheeled barrel organs; they fell into the hands of indifferent owners and went to pieces. How unnoticed and unmourned was their passing! There was one peg organ which met its end in quite a spectacular way, however. It had been rented to the Hagenbeck Circus, where an elephant was supposed to crank it with its trunk. But the elephant did not seem to care for this kind of music. When he brought his mighty foot down on this little organ, the instrument gave its last pitful sob; this may well have been the lowest point of the performance!

THE ORIGIN OF THE BOOK ORGAN

Although the building of the first book organ by Gavioli in 1892 came as a surprise and unleashed a true revolution in the organ world, in reality it was the culmination of a series of events which had more or less cleared the way for Gavioli. Now (as a hindsight) it could be considered inevitable.

In the chapter on reed organs we have already described how in 1712 the automatic weaving loom was invented by Joseph Jacquard, whereby the design of the fabric was punched out in cardboard; in 1842 a patent was given A. F. Seytre for an application of the same principle in the playing of musical instruments; in 1861 the first "Kartonium" was built by J. A. Teste, functioning on the same principle; and how, after that, key claviers and perforated cardboard were used in all sorts of reed organs and string instruments.

Therefore, it is not only the application of the book system to organ building, but also the beautiful results he had with his new format, for which he merits the greatest possible homage and admiration. The brilliant success of these book organs was quite unexpected. In reed organs and string instruments, the book system was welcome because it opened the way to an unlimited expansion of the repertoire, but it did not result in any important change in the music or character of the sound of these instruments. That the latter was very definitely the case with the Gavioli-built book organs, was due not only to the book system as such, but also to the fact that he improved his product significantly in two more ways. In the first place, he built the new instruments according to the pneumatic system, the principle of which he borrowed from church organ construction; and secondly, he supplied certain registers with the so-called "frein harmonique" (harmonic brake) developed by him and patented in 1878. About the "harmonic brake" we can say this: of the many kinds of wooden flutes which are used in the street organ, certain narrow-scaled ranks are designed to imitate a string instrument (violin, celeste, cello, unda maris, etc.). The "brake" consists of a small metal plate, bent at an acute angle, attached to the pipe in such a way that it enters the air stream at the mouth and produces a full string sound. The tone-color of flutes fitted with the brake gains considerably in richness.

Because of the three mentioned factors, the book system, the pneumatic system, and the harmonic brake (the first two of which brought about a great improvement in organ construction), it was possible to construct organs which differed so strikingly in tone quality from the cylinder type that J. W. Enschede says: "The street organ changed from a wind-sick beggars' instrument to the excellent instrument which graces our streets with its fresh, clear tones." Of course, we must not forget that several factors contributed to this unfavorable comparison, beyond the inherent characteristics of the barrel organ itself. In the first place, "new items" usually enjoy a wave of popularity to the detriment of the old-fashioned ones, and secondly, new instruments of any sort generally function better than those which have been in service for years. This latter factor especially played an important part in the disfavor of the old barrel organs. We shall go into this later.

However, before we go into this comparison between the new and the old street organs, we must find out what was responsible for the appearance of the new book organs in our streets. The first point to understand is that in the first years after 1892, the book organs were built exclusively for fairs and dancing. When Gavioli started constructing the new instrument, he certainly never envisioned it as the new street organ. On the contrary, the really important customers, to whom he geared his production, were the taverns and fair concessions. We shall return in chapter 9 to the demands of the former category in particular. The fact that book organs in both forms of entertainment, fair and dance organs . . . were an immediate success was due not only to the better quality of the music, but also to the larger dimensions which the instruments assumed, thanks to the book clavier and the pneumatic system. In the barrel organ the number of keys was dependent on the length of the cylinder, but the pneumatic book organ could contain many more keys without becoming too clumsy and long. This was so because in the new claviers, the keys could be closer together than they could where a cylinder was concerned, in which case the wire pins and bridges of all the tunes not being played had to have room enough to pass in between the keys without engaging them, while only the tune which had been selected to play was in direct line with the keys. The combination of folding books and a pneumatic system encouraged the addition of a choice collection of different registers.

The first result of the resounding success of the book organ for fairs and dance halls was that many other organ

Ludovic Gavioli II.

factories copied the discoveries of Gavioli and it did not take long for book organs to be seen everywhere. From the following survey of factories and shops where book organs were constructed at the beginning of this century, it will be clear to what an extent this new industry grew, first in France and shortly after also in Belgium and Germany.

In France were the thriving factories of Gavioli, Gasparini (also Italians who settled in France), Marenghi, and Limonaire Freres, and also Poirot Freres and Remy & Grobert who have already been mentioned in chapter 3.

In Belgium and equally thriving were Fassano, de Vreese, Koeningsberger, Burssens, De Cap, Mortier, Hooghuys, Dewijn, Steenput, Pierre Verbeeck, Daneels, and others.

During this same time the fair organ industry reigned supreme in Germany. We make special mention of Bruder, Ruth, Wellershaus, Richter, Wrede, and Voigt. In most cases, many members of these families were in the concern and succeeded each other from generation to generation.

In the next chapters we shall go more thoroughly into the various kinds of organs made by these French, Belgian, and German builders and into the great influence of the French and Belgian ones in particular on the further development of the pierement in the Netherlands.

The Introduction of the Street Book Organs, or "Pierement", in the Netherlands.

It was quite predictable that in view of the signal victory of the new organs at fairs and in the dance halls that Leon Warnies should have the idea of commissioning similar organs for his street organ concern, and his initiative certainly does not detract from the very special place he occupies in the history of "pierementology", for it was he alone who laid the groundwork for the further evolution of the street book organ in the Netherlands. If there ever were concerns abroad where one could rent street organs, they surely must have disappeared with the old barrel organs. It seems to us more likely, however, that the instruments which were used on the streets abroad belonged to the users themselves. Unfortunately, the position of these foreign street musicians became increasingly unpleasant after the revolution in organ building which Anselme Gavioli initiated in 1892. During the time when barrel organs were made on a large scale by organ builders, in various price ranges depending on the size of the belly, peg, or cart-type organ, it was possible for a man to finance one himself. However, when the manufacturers began to specialize more and more on folding book machines, in order to meet the mushrooming demand from fair concessionnaires, innkeepers and street organ licensees, with the result that they limited their varieties of cylinder organs increasingly and finally stopped production altogether, the foreign street musicians were left out in the cold. The large new organs were far too costly for them to purchase, and cylinder organs were to be had only second hand, if it all, so they were forced to go out with old instruments which gradually depreciated. Buchner speaks of these old cylinder organs as "a horror and the bad conscience of society".

We still have not explained why the development of the street organ ran a positive course in Holland after the 19th century, while the opposite happened in all other countries. Why did business-like renting concerns like Warnies' spring up in the Netherlands but not in other countries? Why did others in our country follow his example, after his obvious success, while none ever did in other countries? We could phrase this question differently. Suppose that there had been such agencies elsewhere, and that they had rented the same organs under the same conditions; would they have met with less success? Unfortunately, the answer will always be more or less a moot point. Still, we believe it should be in the affirmative. Warnies, and the other Dutch concerns, owed their success, according to our way of thinking, not only to the two factors we have already mentioned . . . the order which was created in the organ world by the regular renting out of organs to permanent license holders and the completely different character of the new book organs as opposed to the traditional barrel type, but also to a third element which we feel has figured significantly in the course the story of the pierement has taken: the great love and interest the Dutch have shown for street organs from the beginning. (Do you remember what we wrote on this subject at the beginning of chapter 6?) This was obvious shortly after Warnies began his rental agency; in other words, during the time that cylinder organs were in their prime and had their chances of success in other countries. Because of the appreciation and sympathy which appeared to exist for the pierement in Holland, a sort of mutual reaction, or interaction developed. Warnies and his successors were encouraged to order more and more organs of more beautiful styles, which in turn influenced the interest of the public in a positive way. Because of this reciprocal effect, the pierement began to assume an ever-greater role in the life of the people, which again had the effect of causing those who were not naturally inclined towards street organ music to begin to respect the pierement as a valuable part of the country's folklore. Thus, the whole Dutch people came to love the instrument . . . some primarily for the music; others for the aesthetic-folkloristic value it had taken on, and because it increased the cheerful and quaint atmosphere of our towns, incidentally making them more attractive to tourists. Thus the pierement became to the Dutch what the bagpipe is to the Scots, the gamelan to the Indonesians, and the balalaika to the Russians, but also what our windmills and carillon towers already meant to us.

But let us return to Warnies and investigate how he laid the foundation for further development of the pierement by introducing the book organ to his clientele. Warnies, and gradually more and more after him (for whenever an enterprise meets with success, competitors spring up), formed the commercially indispensable financial link between the organ builders on the one hand and the renters on the other. Because of this position, the Dutch organ renters gave the deciding impetus to the production of street organs destined for Holland by foreign manufacturers. This impetus worked favorably in another quarter also: the social standing of the organ grinder was much improved. The pierementologist J. W. Enschede has this to say on the subject: "He is no longer the beggar of former times; the Savoyard, travelling about with his hurdy-gurdy and his marmot (an animal like the woodchuck or ground hog). The Amsterdam organ man of today has a higher position, which can best be described as that of a disabled laborer who is fairly well off . . . it is said that one of them is a retired navy officer! The improvement in the sound and technique of the organs themselves is echoed in the personnel connected with them." There is no doubt that this change in status of the organ players played an important role in the course street music took in the Netherlands as opposed to other countries.

Judging from observations which we ourselves have made, we think that the improvement of the social position of the organ-renter mentioned by Enschede must have been another case of interaction. In presenting this idea, we should like to liven up things a bit by using some of the vernacular of the organ circles instead of the precisely accurate, standard vocabulary we should have to cling to if we were compelled to be perfectly pedagogical. For instance, "meegeven" is used instead of the less colorful "rent", and "neerzetten" means to terminate a contract. "Mansen" expresses the idea of paying for services rendered, and a "ploeg" is a lessee of an organ. But now to our second case of mutual reaction. Suppose there is a rumor that the organ lessor plans to put a brand-new instrument on the streets. He turns it over to the "ploeg" who most deserves such an instrument, in his estimation. (A "ploeg" is deemed worthy of a good instrument if he cares for it conscientiously, cleaning it, covering it with a canvas when it rains, not leaving it outside at night, being careful with it in traffic, keeping vandals away from it, and paying the rent promptly.) The "ploeg" who gets the organ and in return, tries to do his best with it, will prove successful. His fellow organ-grinders, convinced that they are just as worthy as he is, do their utmost to get at least a comparable instrument. The organ companies (especially the competitors of the one we are discussing!) thus are compelled to put new organs, and if possible more beautiful ones, into circulation. As soon as such a new instrument arrives and has been prepared for the street, the "ploeg" who is taking it leaves his old one, after which the agency may decide to have it rebuilt in the new style. And what is the outcome of all this? Because of the success of the new organs, the lessors begin to raise their standards, so that men who formerly would have been ashamed to make their living playing a street organ now are attracted to the profession, They find that it now conforms adequately to their social standards and they are happy to share in the admiration which the organ grinders reap with their music. Thus the guild of organ grinders is swelled with new and desirable license holders. On the other hand, those who cannot or will not keep up with the most enterprising individuals and still possess only old and outdated organs will be inclined to discontinue their profession.

From this we see how organ manufacturers and renters have progressed as a result of Leon Warnie's initiative: the builders through the evolution of the new type of street organ using the book system, and the renters through the elevation of their status because of association with these beautiful new instruments.

This is the story of how the book organs forced the barrel organs off the streets, first in Amsterdam, during the first 25 years of the 20th century. Unfortunately, old Leon Warnies did not live to see the arrival of his first order of book organs, for he died shortly before they were to be delivered . . . in December, 1902. His business was continued by his widow, however. Next to her concern, which was still located at the original address in the Brouwersgracht, a new rental agency was started by two of Leon's sons, Leon and Gabriel, under the name "Warnies Brothers" (Gebroeders Warnies). In Rotterdam the rental agents Van Eerdenburg and Goudswaard continued with the original barrel organs. In 1911 Louis Holvoet, a disciple of Warnies, settled in the city and became famous, for it was he who introduced the book organ to Rotterdam. Thus began the triumph of the pierement there. Inevitably the book organ replaced the old cylinder instruments everywhere in the Netherlands.

Our conclusion is that the question we posed at the beginning of this chapter can be answered completely in the affirmative. Rightly, the pierement is called a typically Dutch musical instrument, notwithstanding the remarkable circumstance that . . . at least until 1920 . . . all street organs were foreign-made, for they were all built with Holland as their destination! It was only here in the Netherlands that the rental of street organs blossomed; only here that the pierement evoked a wave of enthusiasm from the lovers of this kind of music. While the public as a whole did not look solely to the pierement for the satisfaction of its musical desires, still there was a more or less universal appreciation of the enrichment of our Dutch folklore and tradition by these instruments, which visually as well as audibly gave a uniquely Dutch flavor to our towns. And this is how the pierement was born and grew in the Netherlands, and how these magnificent organs came to occupy a niche all their own in the life of our nation. They belong to us . . . we cannot and will not live without our pierement!

The Pierement in the Twenties

8

In order to understand completely the gradual development of the street organ as a type apart from fair and dance organs, first we can profit from an explanation of the characteristics each of these has in view of its ultimate use. The dance organ is distinguished by the strongly accented rhythm of its music: the many short, powerful chords of the heavy and dark-sounding registers simply forced the dancing couples to maintain the correct rhythm. A choice collection of percussion instruments . . . large drum with or without cymbals, small drum, clappers (two straight pieces of wood used like castanets and called "bones" in negro minstrels), castanets, triangle, etc. . . . serve to bring out the differences in nuance between the stronger and the weaker parts of the measures.

The dimensions of these dance organs are often enormous, partly due to the great number of registers, or stops. I have here in front of me the stoplist [1] of a Mortier organ with 101 keys. Excluding the basses, trombones, and accompaniment, I find here as registers for melody: violin piano, violin forte, unda maris, flute harmonique, baxophone, xylophone, jazz flute, piston and fibration; as harmony: cello, celeste, bariton, bass cello, flute 8, pifaro and bassoon; as percussion: large and small drum, cymbals, clappers, a triangle, and three bells. But aside from the pipework and all the necessary mechanical parts, there was another reason why these monumental instruments grew to

---

1. Survey of the various tonal qualities of the different stops as they correspond to the keys of the mechanism.

nine metres in length and six metres in height. This was the purely visual need to have the organ case fill an entire wall of the dance hall, which led to the building of extra side and top pieces apart from the main section, which contained most of the registers, the mechanism, and the bellows. The more or less incidental registers, as well as the percussion groups or some of the purely mechanical parts of the instrument were housed in these additional cases. Often accordions were built into the dance organ. As registers which played a part in the appearance of the instrument, we mention the flute harmonique and bass cello. These consisted, in contrast with most of the other registers which were basically wooden flutes, of metal pipes which were painted decoratively. The flute harmonique was placed in the lower center (referred to as the "buik", or abdomen), while the very large bass cello pipes were placed in the special side chests, to the left and right of the main central case.

The fair organs differed from the dance organs particularly in the much stronger and sharper sound, in which the upper registers were prominent. Here the accent was not on the heavy, booming chords or pronounced rhythmic accents, but rather on the melody, which emerged with a clear, radiant sound, executed by soft-sounding violin parts which were augmented during the forte passages by fresh-sounding mixtures. The counter-melody was of a full and sonorous timbre; in the German organs from the trumpets, in the French and Belgian, baritones. In some makes, for example Gavioli and Gasparini, all this was bathed in a piccolo obligatto, sometimes combined with a glockenspiel constructed of steel plates, also called "metallophone".

The wide, majestic front of a fair organ.

The different kinds of fair organs differed greatly in size. In the small merry-go-rounds for children often very small but valiant . . . sometimes even saucy! . . . organs did their best. The opposite extreme were the large concert organs built into separate fair wagons and functioning as pace-setters in large establishments, such as the steam carousels and shimmy palaces. In this field one thinks of Wolfs, Hommerson, Vermolen, Janvier, Benner, etc. This is the place to call attention to the fact that many French and Belgian organ builders, after the example of Gavioli, tuned their instruments one and a half steps higher (a minor third) than normal to obtain a more brilliant sound. Thus they were not tuned in C but in E flat, and the notes which were labelled C actually were E flat. Later Carl Frei, of whom more follows, did the same with the street organs he built and rebuilt. The German manufacturers, however, steadfastly tuned their instruments in C. Their product differed in another respect from the French and Belgian ones in that they used a tracker bar working pneumatically instead of a mechanical key clavier. Round holes the same size as those in the tracker bar were punched in the music; for held notes, many holes in succession. In the books for key claviers long rectangular holes are made of the necessary width to allow the key to slip up into the corresponding groove in the copper roll above, and of just the right length for the precise amount of time required by the composition.

To return to the beginning: the street organ differed from the dance and fair instruments especially in the more lyrical and sensitive character of the music, and of course in its smaller size. While the latter two categories could be powered by motors, the pierement had to be cranked by hand, which meant that the bellows could not be too large or heavy. The number of registers and pipes was subject to a certain degree of limitation also. Then the organs had to be of a manageable size for the renters to take through the streets. In Amsterdam in particular consideration had to be given to the sometimes very high bridges which would have to be negotiated.

Besides the dance, fair, and street organs with their individual characteristics, there are all sorts of transitional types. This is understandable in light of the fact that street organs were built by manufacturers who originally made fair and dance organs. The German organ factories produced mostly fair organs, the French both fair and dance instruments; Belgium was always the country par excellence of dance organs, both in production and in sales, although this does not mean that they never turned out any good fair organs. We think, on this subject, of the big fair organ, "De Cap", which is known under the name of "Falco", and of the Hooghuijs fair organs. Several records are now commercially available of one of these last.

Considering the pierement, originally it was mainly Gasparini and, after 1910, Limonaire Freres who supplied the Netherlands with street organs. Later on the Belgian factories of Burssens, De Vreese, and eventually De Cap came into the picture.

The old cylinder street organs were mostly German, one of the most well-known of these being Wellerhaus. It is remarkable that there were very few book organs supplied directly by the German manufacturers as such, but it does appear that the few originally booksystem organs which came from Germany at the beginning of this century were of very good quality. For example, there are the "Bruder" organs "De Bazuin" (The Trumpet), "De Bloempot" (The Flowerpot), and "De Reuzenkast" (The Giant Case) all using books with round perforations and pneumatic tracker bars as was typical of German instruments. It happened much more often, however, that German cylinder organs were rebuilt by French and Belgian organ factories into book organs. A number of our present pierement are instruments which originally contained barrels. With the exception of the few original German book organs which we mentioned above, all pierement were built with the mechanical key clavier.

It is time to return to the time of the very first book organs and to tell something about their music and outward appearance. We must assume that none of these old instruments has been kept in exactly the same form it was in when it arrived in the Netherlands new from the factory. Would you like to know approximately how these early organs sounded? Then just visit the museum "Van speeldos tot pierement" at Utrecht and you can listen to the so-called "Aalster Gavioli". This organ was carefully kept by Mr. Pierre van Roy at Aalst in the same state as Gavioli built it about 1900. It was taken to the museum at Utrecht on May 23, 1957 and there was rebaptized as "The Aalster Gavioli" (see picture). The collection of book music which belongs to this organ dates back to 1904. It was originally built as a dance organ, which is apparent in the very high top and the extra side cases with carving placed next to the side cases with the drums. If one were to imagine the organ with the top and the side pieces gone, then it would measure up perfectly to all the standards of a good street book organ at the beginning of this century. The mechanism has sixty-seven keys, and the registers for melody are violin and piccolo; those for counter-melody, baritone and clarinet. Neither the piccolos (which are typical of Gasparini pierement) nor the clarinets are nowadays found in street organs. In the case of the clarinets, this is due to the fact that this register consisted partially of brass pipes which went out of tune easily due to changes in the weather. The

"The Aalster Gavioli". In the middle, front, the violins; left and right in front, the piccolos; behind the piccolos, the baritones; entirely in the back, the brass pipes of the clarinets.

frequent temperature changes to which a street organ is constantly subjected wreaked havoc with them. Furthermore, they were also reed pipes, which made them a double tuning risk. Another register which was well-known and a favorite in the years 1910-1920 disappeared for the same reason, the so-called "vox humana" popularly called "human voice" or just "voice" for short. It also consisted partially of brass reed pipes and it had a strong vibrato produced by a tremulant device which constantly interrupted the supply of air and permitted it to flow again, alternating the two at a great rate of speed. In this way a unique sound was created of such a special quality that it was likened to the human voice. The tendency to endow the organs with personalities of their own probably contributed to this comparison.

This tendency also led to the christening of each instrument with a name of its own. These names were selected with the greatest ingenuity, as is readily apparent in the following collection from famous organs of the past and present. Often organs were named because of size or color, as with "Het Blauwtje" (Little Blue), "Het Witje" (Little White), "De grote Witte" (Big White); sometimes because of the characteristics of the facade, as in "De grote Buik" (Big Belly), "De kleine Buik" (Little Belly), "Het gouwe Kappie" (Gold Top), and "De Puntkap" (Pointed Top). Occasionally they owed their names to the carving, as with "De Turk" (The Turk), or to the figures painted on the side panels of the facade, as in "De Arabier" (The Arab), and "De Bloemenmeid" (The Flower Girl). It also happened that the name of the manufacturer or the number of keys in the clavier influenced the choice: "De blauwe Gasparini" (Blue Gasparini), "De Negentiger" (Ninety Key), "De 54 Burssens" (54 Burssens). The character of the music sometimes dictated the choice; for example, "Het Huilebalkie" (Cry Baby) and "Het Snotneusje" (Snot-Nose), a very small organ which, however, could hold its own along with its big brothers and sisters and sang along valiantly. Once in a great while a special event figured in the name, like "Het Waterduikertje" (The Diver), which once took a dive into the water, or a special characteristic influenced the choice, as in "De Cementmolen" (The Cement Mill), whose wheel was extra big. It also occurred that the name came from the man who played it, as was the case with "De Pod", which remained for years in the hands of the well-known Amsterdamian, Jan de Pod.

Many organgrinders themselves have nicknames. At the beginning of this century the people of Amsterdam were familiar with "Lange Jan" (Long John), who became famous mainly because he was the first one to appear (in 1903) with a book organ in the streets; then there were "Sleepbeen" (Lame Leg), "Magere Bertus" (Lean Bert), "Lange Hein" (Long Henry), "De Boomaap" (Tree Ape), "Mossenessie" (Mossy Essie), and his spouse, "Tante Heintje" (Aunt Hendrika). In the following chapters we shall meet a number of well-known figures from the world of the street organ of this era.

Now, however, we want to return to our story about the earliest book organs, which we abandoned temporarily because of our digression over the vox humana. Besides the already-mentioned registers of violin, piccolo, vox humana, clarinet, and baritone, the frequently-encountered xylophone deserves our attention. This consisted of a series of tuned wooden bars hung in the opening in the middle of the facade and played by small wooden mallets. This register could also be used in slow melodies with long held notes; in this case the same mallets would hit the wood bars repeatedly in fast tempo in a vibrating effect.

It is not without a certain amount of pleasure that we use this opening to recall a quite remarkable sort of organ, one which attracted much attention from among the many types that were on the streets, the so-called "bottle organ", or "bouteillophone" as the French termed it. In these instruments was installed a special register of eleven tuned bottles, played with mallets just like the xylophone. Unfortunately, there was to be no great future in store for these organs. Even after only a few short years, they have completely disappeared from the scene and there is not even one of them left now, probably due to the special manner in which they had to be tuned. In order to give the bottles the right pitch, one had to fill them very carefully to a certain height with a liquid . . . and no ordinary water could be used! In order to procure a pure, true tone, the bottles had to be filled to the required height with the noblest essence known in street organ circles . . alcohol. It is easy to imagine that certain of the musicians, ever conscientiously striving for a perfectly-tuned instrument, found it imperative to tune the bottles themselves from time to time. In the process they always seemed to notice that one or more of the bottles was just a little too low in tone because it contained a trifle too much alcohol. If, while busily tuning, they accidentally extracted too much and the bottle became sharp-sounding compared to the others which had not been "tuned", then of course this defect had to be corrected immediately. All the other bottles also had to be tuned higher, of course by removing some of the contents. You will remark that in that case, the whole stop would be too high compared with the other registers. Naturally! But by this time the "tuners" had become so engrossed with their tuning fever that they no longer perceived this discrepancy; and furthermore, when the police stepped in to maintain law and order, they would argue with them so violently in defense of their tuning procedures, that the whole thing finally ended in the general prohibition of musical bottles in street organs.

We can assure you from our own experience that organ grinders . . . especially under the circumstances we have just outlined . . . are only too ready to begin an emotional debate with anyone who dares dispute their well-considered opinion on any "pierementological" subject. It is also true that the Amsterdam police were just as ready to reciprocate with blanket prohibitions when individuals violated the ordinances designed to regulate their activities. It is better to consider this tale of the fall of the bottle organs as an example of what *could* happen in the street organ world . . . considering the temperament of its inhabitants . . . rather than an established precedent.

Finally we wish to devote our attention to the outward appearance of the book organs from 1900 to 1920. One first notices that most of them are supplied with three carved figures placed in the open center section. The middle figure was the conductor . . . called "kapelmeester" on the scale of the book . . . who held a small baton in his right hand and beat time with it to the rhythm of the music. Moreover, he moved his head and left arm at the switch from loud to soft registers and vice versa. On either side he usually had a charming young lady, each holding a small bell in one hand and grasping in the other a mallet with which to strike it, usually simultaneously with the big drum and cymbals. All these movements were made possible by small bellows placed inside the arms, whose position changed according to whether or not there was air pressure in the bellows. These bellows were controlled by the mechanism of the organ, and the composer of the books determined not only the arrangement, but also the movements of the statues. On some organs the ladies distinguished themselves from their colleagues by doing a pirouette while the music played. For this the skirts were constructed in such a manner that one would have thought the dancers were wearing real petticoats.

The top piece of "De Bels" (The Belgian) as it appears at present in the Perlee shed in Amsterdam.

Not only in respect to the carved figures, but also in other features the fronts of these early organs were very elegant. Of course, every factory had its own style, but in general swirls and curlicues predominated. Much attention was paid even to the details of the front carving, such as the drum cases and the pillars, into which female heads were carved. Of this, very little is left. Fortunately, the most beautiful top (the part of the front that extends above the case proper) of one of the oldest and most famous book organs has been preserved: the top of the organ, "De Bels" (The Belgian). It may be seen in the shed of the rental agent Perlee in the Westerstraat in Amsterdam. It got its name through having come to Holland via Belgium. "De Bels", a creation of the French organ builders Limonaire Freres, was especially famous for its beautiful vox humana and first played on the street in Amsterdam by the well-known "Lange Jan" (Long John), who often had the new organs first. Unfortunately, the facade of "De Bels" was eventually destroyed by fire, the fine top piece alone surviving. The instrument itself was largely saved and after being rebuilt, now serves as a fair organ.

We could not end this examination of the outward appearance of the early book organs without telling you something about the colors in which they were generally painted.

Everyone nowadays thinks it only normal that the big center case be painted brown, with the two side cases which jut out on either side of the deeper center case in a lighter color, often pale green or pale blue and the facade, placed in front of the whole case and usually including a top which extends over the center case and the side extensions as well, in a combination of many light colors. Often the background of the front is pink or cream color, and the scrolls and flourishes embellishing it are usually done in silver with varied color hues overlaid. Sometimes gold leaf is used on the facade. Names like "De Gouwe" (The Golden One), and "Het Gouwe Kappie" (The Golden Top) remind us of this fact. This method of painting dates back to the period of the first book organs. There has not always been unanimity of opinion on this subject. The "Circle of Street Organ Friends" has in its archives old photographs in which one may see book organs by Poirot Freres which are black in front, or at least very dark. It is known that the firm of Wellershaus, for one, painted its cylinder street organs dark. When the well-known painter of organ facades, Jan Bal, who painted for Dutch organ agencies all his life, once painted a Wellershaus cylinder organ in light colors just as an experiment, he was so enthusiastic about the effect that since then he has painted all his organs in light colors, not only the fronts, but the back cases as well. We presume that with most of our readers it is the old cylinder organs that live on in memory, their cases painted freshly white. This, then, is the explanation. The big center cases of the book organs have since then been given a more neutral and less eye-catching brown color, but the contrasting fronts remain mostly light in color, while the same goes for the side cases.

In summing up our impressions of the character of the book organ in the first twenty years of this century, we give first place to the fact that they sounded sweeter and more sensitive than the shriller-sounding cylinder organs, in which the mixtures and trumpets were far too dominant. On the other hand, these early book organs still sounded completely different from what we are used to in the piere-ment of today. As we have seen, this stems from the fact that many of the old registers have disappeared from the instruments to be replaced by others. Furthermore, before 1920 the arrangements were much simpler, for the composers of that time did not know how to take the fullest advantage of the musical capacities of the organs. However beautiful the old "vox humana" organs, and however interesting the bottle stop, the music of that era was usually limited to a simple melody against a background of basses and accompaniments which only accentuated the rhythm and filled out the harmony. All this changed radically, however, when in 1920 the organ builder, arranger, and composer of street organ music, Carl Frei, settled in Breda (a small town in the south of the Netherlands). He was the first to demonstrate what surprising results can be achieved when the artistry of the arranger and composer of street organ music rests on four pillars: complete control of harmony and counterpoint, or composition; a thorough knowledge of all the musical secrets of each individual organ; a creative mind and great musical imagination; and an outspoken love for the instrument! It was Carl Frei who brought to the zenith of perfection the art of creating a professional arrangement which presented in turn ebullient cheerfulness impish playfulness, lacy refinement, tender sensitivity, and heavy melancholy. He accomplished this by artfully using fast and crystal-clear "waterfalls" (glissandos), witty and gossipy ornaments in the form of trills and grace notes, and martial chords to provide the proper contrast. All this was more or less tied together by a quiet but purposeful harmony of heavy registers. Some-

"De Turk" *(The Turk)* *as it now appears in use in Loosduinen.*

141

times a sentimental melody in a hypersensitive register . . . which made the organ grinder feel like crying . . . was bathed in a chatter of joking piccolos which gave an arresting, piquant quality to the music. Or again, a main melody arranged in saucy, pert chords stood out against the melancholy background of a sentimental, wistful accompaniment. Throughout all this the percussion and short, powerful trombone blasts used to augment the ground basses furnished the necessary accents at just the right moments.

If you would like to hear for yourself the differences between the music of the older book organs and the arrangements which Carl Frei made after 1920, you can listen to a record of an old "vox humana" organ and one of the first marches which Frei composed in the twenties and arranged for book organs, which had already been on the Amsterdam streets since 1910. We refer to the march "Molto Vivace" on the organ "De Turk". After listening to this record, you will understand our effusions over the Carl Frei arrangements. Besides the "Aalster Gavioli", which we mentioned on page 132, "De Turk" is the only old book organ which still has the same registers as were built into it during a remodelling job done before the first World War. It is the only organ still in use in our country in which there still remains a piccolo register. This famous organ may be heard Saturday afternoons at Loosduinen (a small village on the coast near the Hague). It will give you a taste of the music as it must have sounded from 1900 to about 1920. Thus we conclude this phase of our story.

The Development of the Pierement in the Period 1920-1940 9

Life around street organs, their players and their enthusiasts, has always been very lively and emotional. Whenever a group of organ fans congregates, discussions always ensue about the qualities of the various organs or the capacities of this or that organ builder or composer. Such subjects are then debated with passionate enthusiasm and sharp criticisms. But however violent these discussions may be, and however intensely opinions may collide, there is one point on which all these enthusiasts always agree completely: the high point in the history of the pierement was reached in the period between 1920-1940. In no other period of the same length did so many new organs appear on the scene with such a richly varied wealth of sound and beauty of appearance. Of course, the increasing popularity which the pierement enjoyed in this period of growth is closely associated with the fact that the book organs imported from France, with their sensitive music, had already conquered so many hearts during the preceding period (1900-1920). That the growing demand for new types of pierement could be met so well in the years 1920-1940 we owe mainly to the Belgian manufacturers and to Carl Frei living in Breda.

Most of the organs which are still in existence today were built by them. In this chapter we wish first to discuss the work and the great merit of these organ builders. Then we shall delve into the disposition and the sound character of the organs of this period, and analyze the difference between the original Belgian organs and those of Carl Frei.

Finally, we shall sketch the atmosphere and environment of the organs in the thirties, at which time we hope to unveil more about the psychological and sociological aspects of lives centered about street organs.

The Belgian Organ Industry

However delightful the development of the organ business as a whole in the twenties and thirties may have been, in one respect we feel a certain melancholy when we think back to this period. This sadness is caused by the fate of the French organ builder, for the French organ industry, to which we owe the invention of the book organ and the revolutionary development of the industry of fair, dance, and street organs around the turn of the century, began to decline shortly afterwards. It appeared that the builders in France could not maintain the fight against the competition of the Belgian organ industry which was developing rapidly at the beginning of the twentieth century. Finally they lost the battle altogether.

What were the causes of this dramatic development? We can gain some insight into it from a comparison of two of the major organ companies, one of them the "Societe Gavioli & Cie" as we know it from the letters of Miss Andree Gavioli to Henri Bank, and the other the dance organ factory of Th. Mortier in Antwerp, of which our Belgian organ friend Th. de Meerleer has supplied us with interesting data.

Miss Gavioli writes about her great-grandfather, Ludovic Gavioli I, who moved the organ factory from Modena, Italy to Paris in 1845; about her grandfather, Anselme Gavioli, who introduced the book organ in 1892; and about her father, Ludovic Gavioli II, a sensitive organ builder and composer, who continued the business after the death of Anselme in 1902. What we read is not only interesting but also moving, for it is obvious from these letters that the Gaviolis were sensitive and ingenious artists, but far from hard-boiled and shrewd business people. About Ludovic I, we read that his good heart moved him to give a beautiful mechanical musical instrument which he had created, portraying King David playing a real harp, to a woman who was some sort of travelling fair concessionnaire. Unfortunately, in spite of solemn promises to return the piece, she disappeared forever with it. Just as heart-breaking was another incident involving a Russian adventurer to whom he entrusted his "Panharmonico" in an effort to sell it, and of whom he saw no more than he did of the woman with the harp. He had been commissioned to build this large orchestrion by the duke of Modena, who desired him to build an instrument that would "surpass all previous ones in sound and ingenuity". When Ludovic had carried out this commission to the full satisfaction of the duke, this miserable man refused to pay for the instrument. An even heavier blow struck when he entrusted his third son, Claude, with the management of the organ factory. A bookkeeper embezzled such enormous amounts that Ludovic was forced to seek financial aid, which he was able to secure only by allying himself with a certain Yver, who did not have the foggiest notion of organ building. This liaison came about in 1861. Two years later Anselme became the manager of the factory, but he also suffered serious setbacks from painfully bad luck. During the war of 1870, when the factory had been moved temporarily to the Elzas, everything was completely destroyed, so that it was necessary to begin all over again. In spite of all this, Anselme managed to build up a flourishing business after the war in Paris with his sensational new inventions (see page 117) and even more so with the business potential he developed by training a select group of specialists in organ building and pipe voicing and tuning. But, alas, a new blow . . . and this time, one from which the ill-fated Gavioli would never completely recover . . . followed in 1901. In that year, such an enormous and fundamental reconstruction of the buildings on the corner of Rue de Bercy and the Quai de la Rapee was found to be necessary (among other things occasioned by the poor condition of the foundation) that practically the entire capital of the Societie had to be invetsed just in the repairs. One of the repercussions was that the travelling expenses of the staff could no longer be paid, and the best and most specialized technicians resigned consequently. One of these specialists, a foreman named Charles Marenghi, who had been initiated into all the secrets of the art of organ building unreservedly by Anselme, even started a competitive business with a group of formerly employed specialists from Gavioli.

The most dramatic aspect of this sad story is that it was just at this time that the new book organs were such a resounding success in the Belgian dance halls, and that Gavioli could not keep up with the ever-growing number of orders. The situation became even worse as the Belgian clients began to demand customized work until the point was reached where each desired his own distinctive style. Neither Gavioli nor the other French organ manufacturers could meet such excessive demands completely. Finally Gavioli, Gasparini, and Marenghi decided to build only one standard type of organ, which would be considerably lower in cost since not every instrument would have to be individually designed and built. Miss Gavioli writes that one French factory . . . this must have been the Limonaire works . . . did not want to go along with this unification "hoping to be able to compete and possibly later to make profits from the leftovers of the once great Gavioli & Cie". The subsequent history of the House of Gavioli tells us that at first this cooperation with the other organ factories resulted in an increase in production, but that eventually the the company went downhill as a consequence of mismanagement by the administrators, laymen in the field of organ building, who had more and more to say in the policies and decisions of the concern. The resistance of Ludovic II had no effect. When eventually in opposition to the bylaws poor quality vacuum cleaners were being manufactured instead of organs, Ludovic II resigned. A short while thereafter the entire business was liquidated.

During the same time that the French organ industry had been going through its death throes, the factory of Th. Mortier in Antwerp had been prospering greatly. What stands out in a comparison between the history of Gavioli and that of Th. Mortier is that the latter, in contrast to Gavioli, always had powerful business connections at his disposal right from the very beginning, which enabled him to reach whatever goal he set out to attain financially. The foundation of his company was established in 1890. Mortier, who was then only an innkeeper, became interested in the dance and tavern organ trade quite naturally, for from time to time he ordered from the firm of Gavioli & Cie a new organ for his own tavern. He planned to remain attractive to the public by this strategem, and as we have already seen, it was just at this time that the new style organs did prove to have such great drawing power. Whenever Mortier bought a new instrument, a buyer would have to be found for the old one. Originally, when barrel organs were being built, the organ trade was modest. However, when book organs became fashionable, business flourished to such an extent that Mortier set up a special repair shop. The next step was the building of completely new organs, much to the displeasure of Gavioli. He had agreed to train Mortier's daughter in the arranging of organ books, but only on the condition that Mortier would not build new organs. When eventually Mortier even began using some of Gavioli's patented inventions, that was the limit. Gavioli sued, with the final result that Mortier had to agree to buy twelve organs annually from Gavioli . . . and now comes the tragedy! He was so embroiled in business difficulties that it proved to be utterly impossible for him to fill the orders, so that Mortier's hands were freed. His company flourished to such an extent that after 1918 a new dance organ was turned out every two or three weeks. At that time he employed sixty to eighty people, some of whom were very skillful and were to become famous in their own right, such as father and son Bax, the inventors of the well-known "baxophone" register in dance organs; the musicians Van Wichelen and Eugene Peersman, well-known Belgian arrangers of organ books; the manufacturer of the "blanco" cardboard books, Jozef van der Mueren; the organ builder Remond Duwijn, who was to start his own business in Wilrijk; and last but not least . . . Carl Frei.

In order to give you a breath of the lively atmosphere of the business of dance organs at that time, we print here the recollections of Leonard Grymonprez, another Belgian organ builder, about Ghent, taken from "Het Pierement" of May 1, 1956:

"There was a time when there were an enormous number of organs in Ghent, even if we disregard the countless smaller instruments and consider only the largest ones, placed in a dominating position on the stage of a beautiful hall, inviting one and all to dance to the polkas and mazurkas, the marches and waltzes. It seems that in those days, when people had to work harder and longer and they were not fortified with vitamins, that the blood ran faster through the veins and one could spring about more lithely and sing more spontaneously. It seems like a dream when one's thoughts drift back to the bobbing couples spinning about the shiny, broad dance floor, the happy, healthy-looking crowds humming the beautiful waltz melodies. Now all this is nothing but a fleeting remembrance of a golden era which can never be recaptured. On Saturday afternoons after work one could hear on all sides: "See you at the "Resada", "De Witte Bol" (The White Ball), "De Nieuwe Zaal" (The New Hall), the "Renaissance"," all beautiful and popular dance halls. The organs there were mostly Mortiers of 76, 81, or 86 keys, a very respectable size. Their facades were beautifully carved, and some had been masterfully painted, the silver and gold-leafed arabesques gleaming splendidly against the background of pink, blue, green, or purple. Several of them, especially in the busiest halls, were illuminated in an effective and artistic way with colored lights, and sometimes when most of the main house lights were turned off a unanimous "aaahhh" rose from the crowd. Everyone gazed spellbound at the organ, which was really magnificent. It was like a fairytale castle suddenly looming up out of the darkness. It was quite unique. Then the best dancers would whirl about the floor, and a burst of enthusiastic applause would climax the whole thrilling scene."

The conclusion to be drawn from the above can be no other than the following: Belgium has long been the country par excellence of organs for taverns and dance halls. When these instruments were still being built with cylinders, they were for the most part built by the French manufacturers. However, after the introduction of the book system, the demand for the new instruments became so enormous that a Belgian industry developed to supply the needs of the inn and tavern keepers. When it grew to the point where it was able to meet domestic demands, there was no further need for the French builders, especially when they proved unable to customize their organs to the point desired by their Belgian customers.

When sketching in this way the rapid evolution of the Belgian organ industry, we must not forget that before the Belgians began to follow in Gavioli's footsteps with book organs, they had already been building barrel instruments, even before 1900. The most important of these early organ builders was definitely Louis Hooghuys, who had started building cylinder organs in 1882. Even with this earlier style he had beautiful results. He built not only for inns and dance halls, but also in particular for fairs. (These instruments called in Flemish "foororgels".)

After this lengthy introduction, none of our readers will be surprised to learn that besides Hooghuys, Mortier, and Duwijn, many other Belgian organ factories subsequently mushroomed. We should mention Fassano & Co., which was later on continued by de Vreese; also Koeningsberger, Steenput, Pierre Verbeeck, Daneels, and especially the large factories of Burssens and De Cap in Antwerp and Hoboken respectively. As far as dance organs were concerned, Mortier remained the uncrowned king, but this does not mean that the other companies did not do a great deal of business, a handsome part of which were the street organs destined for the Netherlands!

Thus we return to our starting point and think we have clearly explained that after the first World War Gavioli, Gasparini, and Limonaire organs were no longer imported in large numbers into our country as the business was taken over more and more by De Vreese, De Cap, Pierre Verbeeck, and Burssens pierements. Their plants were much closer to our southern border. However, we do not want to give the impression that all their production was completely new instruments. Certainly there were new ones, especially in the later years, but it also happened that old cylinder organs and old-fashioned French book organs were modernized. In what respect did the new Belgian organ differ from the original French ones? The answer to this question we shall commence on page 156 when we discuss the disposition of the organs of that period, at least as far as the musical side of the subject is concerned, but regarding the exterior of the Belgian product we can now say the following:

1. The carved figures disappeared from the front. Why? In the first place, because people craved change and variety. Another factor was, in our opinion, that the romantic period was at an end and the modern, more objective and businesslike conduct of organ manufacturing was reflected in the decorative effects. The reasoning behind it was as follows: the figures made no music and stood for nothing but maintenance and repairs.

2. In general the number of curlicues, pillars, scrolls, and other ornaments was reduced and the curved lines were replaced by straight or angular ones and planes.

3. In the years around 1930 panels were mounted in front of the side cases of many of the organ facades, especially at De Cap, Pierre Verbeeck, and De Vreese, with approximately life-size figures painted on them. Many organs owe their names to them, for example "De Arabier" (The Arabian), "De Duif" (The Dove . . . a woman holding a dove), "De Bloemenmeid" (The Flower Girl . . . a girl with a bouquet of flowers in her and), and "De Sik" (The Goatee . . . a man with a funny pointed goatee). Later on this practice was again abandoned and these areas were once more decorated in the traditional manner, or, in trade terms, provided with "open carved work".

4. Originally the "flute harmonique" register was usually built into the "buik" ("belly", or lower front center)

An example of the type of pierement in style around 1930 with painted side panels and the flute harmonique register in the "belly". ("buik", or lower front center section)

152

of the dance organ. This consisted of rather thin-sounding flutes (originally made of zinc, or sometimes, wood) with a hole in the center of the pipe, so that it "overblew", that is, sounded an octave higher. Gradually this practice, too, was abandoned. It turned out to be unwise to have the mouths of the pipes so close to the ground, for mischievous youngsters delighted in dropping in sand or gravel!

The Organ Builder Carl Frei

Of the many organ builders to whom we owe the flourishing period in the street organ business between the first and second World Wars, one person in particular draws our attention: Carl Frei, an artist who at that time lived in Breda. Whatever we have written about the Belgian organ industry does not in any way minimize the fact that he should be considered the central figure in the organ world at that time. We have him to thank for the subsequent refinement of the tone color of the street organs . . . and also of many fair organs . . . and it was primarily he who left the stamp of his many-sided artistry on the development of organ music in the period from 1920-1940. The fact that Carl Frei is even now the most beloved and admired organ builder stems from the union in his character of the qualities of acutely sensitive creative musician and artistic organ builder, all bathed in the glow of his noble character, which won all hearts.

The many facets of his talent are apparent in:

1. His many original street-organ compositions, which still represent the most popular part of the repertoire. Who is there who is not acquainted with his poetic, pensive serenades and his romantically-flowing waltzes, which never fail to touch organ lovers? And then, his fresh and well-known, melodious marches! How can it possibly be that

they have never been adopted by our bands and orchestras? At the twenty-three street organ competitions which have been held since 1954, these marches have been the ones most played. How frequently we hear the strains of "Molto vivace", "Hommerson March", "Huzaren-attack" (Hussars' Attack), "Hans Albers March", "Spanienmars" (Spaniards March), "Indische patrouille" (Indian Scouts), "Cinematograaf-mars" (Motion Picture March), "Bredase jongens" (Boys from Breda), "Haagse hopjes" (Coffee Candy), "Groet aan Breda" (Greetings to Breda), "Leve het pierement" (Long Live the Pierement), and many others. Any pierement fan can sing them to you from beginning to end!

2. The sublime arrangements he made for scores of fair and street organs. We call your attention here to our description at the end of chapter 9.

3. His very special knack for harmonious and complementary grouping of the registers chosen for his organs, and also for voicing the pipes. We shall return to this subject later when we take up register combinations and tonal color. You have probably noticed that the characters of Carl Frei and Gavioli and similar in many respects, and possibly you have wondered therefore whether Frei's business and commercial ventures were as pitiful as Gavioli's. Fortunately, we can give you reassurance . . . even though he has let his heart guide him, just as Gavioli did. Significant in this respect is the title of one his most famous serenades, "Het gouden hart" (The Golden Heart). But would this "heart" have provided him with gold had he fortunately not been blessed with a clever Flemish wife, who always knew when it was necessary to be hard-boiled?

The influence of Carl Frei has been such that we feel we owe it to our readers to furnish a short sketch of this master's life. He was born April 4, 1884 in Schidlachin the

Black Forest. After taking lessons in harmony and counter-point from the age of nine at the music academy in Wald-kirch, Bresgau, he began an apprenticeship in the organ factory of "Wilhelm Bruder Sohne", also in Waldkirch, at the age of fourteen. At that time (1898) only cylinder organs were made there. He was not initiated into the secrets of the book organ and the new pneumatic system until 1901, when he started working at the Gavioli branch which had opened in Waldkirch two years previously. About the technical knowledge which Frei accumulated during this period, Henri Bank has this to say in "Het Pierement", May, 1957: "In his spare time this young, in-quisitive organ builder could often be found in one of the inns in the midst of the organ builders of Waldkirch; tip-plers who over a few glasses of beer would become talkative and begin boasting of their trade secrets. The talk was usually about the making and voicing of organ pipes. Not one word slipped by the attentive Carl Frei, when perhaps a certain builder who was famous for the beautiful timbre of his violin pipes was talking about how the mouths, lips, and slits had to be shaped to achieve a special tone-color. Supplied with many technical details, he would repair to his workshop and experiment until he too could make the desired quality of violin pipe. In 1902 Frei moved to Paris to work in the main Gavioli organ works there. How im-portant it must have been for his subsequent development as organ builder and musician to have this regular and personal contact with Ludovic Gavioli II. However, the fact that he was the only German in this company exclu-sively of French, Belgian, and Italian personnel meant that he was to have a difficult time. More than once his fellow workers played practical jokes on him. On one occasion they "accidentally" connected the tubes of a newly-built organ in the wrong order, and when the books composed by Frei were put on, the result was a horrible cacophony. At first Frei was blamed, for of course it was thought he had not done the books properly. He was mystified, because he knew he had studied and taken down the scale of the organ correctly. Fortunately, he was able to locate the "error" and reconnect the tubing in the proper order. This time the music was excellent.

Carl Frei's training was just as many-sided as was his ultimate blossoming into independent composer-arranger-builder. In 1908 he started to work for Th. Mortier, and after that he joined Fassano and De Vreese, in 1910. In 1913 he had the courage to found his own factory, where he built his first complete organ, destined for Jan Griep's restaurant on Dijkstraat in Antwerp. Unfortunately, he could not enjoy his first firm very long . . . the first World War forced him to close his doors, and he had to go to the front where he was seriously wounded. Fortunately, in time he did make a complete recovery.

In 1920 Frei made the decision which was to have such important results for the ultimate development of the automatic organ in the Netherlands. He settled in Breda and began to build up an organ factory on Terheydenseweg, which flourished. The number of commissions to build, rebuild, modernize, and restore organs, and to compose large collections of books for these and other organs increased gratifyingly. At first these commissions came from fair managers, but soon several Amsterdam and Rotterdam street organ agencies followed suit. More about this later. Now it is time to initiate our readers into the musical structure of the Belgian and Carl Frei organs, as they presided over our streets between 1920 and 1940.

Disposition of Registers and Tonal Color

In order to distinguish between the disposition of registers in the various types of street organs which were in use between the first and second World Wars, we must begin by dividing them into two main groups: the smaller organs with only "melody" registers, and the larger ones with both "melody" and "harmony" ranks of pipes. In the ones with only "melody", the pipes may be divided into three groups:

The Bass Group

To this group of pipes belong first of all the so-called ground basses. These are the largest and widest wood pipes of a street organ. (Note here that all pipes discussed will be of wood unless otherwise stated.) If they stood upright, many would stick out above the case. That this does not occur in practice is because these pipes run partially vertically and partially horizontally, since they have been mitered to a 90° angle. This makes no difference to the pitch and the sound quality: the total length of the pipe is the only criterion. Often the ground basses, or at least the mouths of the pipes, are located in the lower section of the organ case. The resulting musical effect is quite satisfactory, because the bass sound comes from "below" in concurrence with the harmonic structure of the music. After all, the basses form the basis on which the music is built! Sometimes the ground basses (16 foot) are augmented by higher basses which sound an octave higher (therefore 8 foot). These ground basses are always stopped pipes; that is, pipes with a wooden stopper in the free end. Higher basses are also usually stopped. For the information of laymen we note that a stopped pipe always sounds an octave lower than an open one. Since the function of the basses is to produce the lowest tones, it follows naturally that they would be stopped.

In many organs the basses can be augmented in forte passages of the music by a special register, the trombones. These are pipes with a powerful, somewhat cracked and trumpet-like sound, shaped like a funnel and supplied with reeds. They are often used together with large drum with cymbal and small drum.

In most organs eight different notes are reserved for the basses, corresponding with the keys for the same notes in the clavier: g, a, b♭, b, c, d, e, and f. In some organs, however, one finds only six bases, the b♭ and the f being omitted, much to the chagrin of the arranger of the music who is now limited in what he can do with the music. Furthermore, we must mention again here that not all organs sound the pitch which is indicated in the scale. Many, including all Gaviolis and most Carl Frei organs, play a minor third higher, as we have already seen, so that one in reality hears an e flat instead of c, etc. There also exist other instruments which transpose upwards more or less than a minor third.

The Accompaniment Group

This group consists exclusively of pipes which serve for musical accompaniment (see sample of music page 165). The accompaniment sounds proportionately soft, because it must not dominate. To this end these pipes are usually situated in the rear of the organ case near the clavier, so that if one should be standing near the back of the organ, and should the panel be open near the clavier (usually this is the case), then the accompaniment will sound too loud. The idea, of course, is to listen to an organ from the front.

Sometimes the accompaniment consists only of a rank of open flutes; sometimes a rank of stopped flutes is added. In this event the tone becomes more radiant and clear, and if desired the accompaniment group could also be used to render a simple harmony which, especially in instruments without a real harmony section, is very attractive.

Strictly speaking, at least 12 notes should be reserved for the accompaniment in the scale of all organs (g, g♯, a, b♭, b, c, c♯, d, e♭, e, f, and f♯), so that any chord needed in a given piece could be obtained. In practice, however, the g♯, the half-step used least often, is almost always lacking, and often the e♭ as well. On the other hand, in some larger organs the number of keys for the accompaniment is greater, so that this group is extended beyond the octave.

The Melody Registers

First, a definition of the concept "register". By this we mean a series, or rank, of organ pipes of the same tone color and timbre. Such a rank of pipes can play by itself or in combination with one or more other ranks, or registers. For each register a separate key has been reserved in the mechanism of the organ for the purpose of switching it on or . . . to use a technical term . . . drawing it. In order to draw a register, also called a "stop" in organ terminology, perforations of approximately one inch in length are punched in the books by the usual process. Other holes have to be punched for the so-called "afsluiter" (lock) or cancel key which simultaneously cancels the registers to be discontinued. The melody proper is brought out by the melody registers, which always sound clear and pronounced as compared to the bass and accompaniment groups. They serve to bring out the music of the so-called "descant" (tune) now in this register, now in another, or in varying combinations. Later on we shall return to the different kinds of song registers. Now we wish to describe the two registers par excellence which are characteristic of organs furnished only with melody: violins and bourdon.

The violins are narrow, open pipes with "frein" (harmonic "brake" . . . see page 117) which produce a fairly strong, biting sound similar to bowing. They are placed in

159

two, three, or sometimes even four rows, so that each note is played on respectively two, three, or four pipes tuned alike, so that they augment each other.

The bourdon is a register that always consists of two rows of closed pipes, wider than the violin, disposed so that two pipes always speak for each note, one of them in front and the other directly behind. Although the listener hears only one note from the two pipes, they are nevertheless not tuned to the same pitch. The pipes in the front row are tuned a few vibrations per second higher than the corresponding ones in the back, with the result that one hears a crystal-clear, fluctuating tone. The number of fluctuations, or beats, per second is identical with the frequency difference between the two pipes, or, as it is popularly expressed: the number of beats one hears in the effect produced by the simultaneous playing of both pipes is the same as the number of vibrations per second the first pipe is tuned higher than the second. In a sense one can compare the wavering sound thus created with the vibrato of a violinist. In both instances the goal is to create an interesting and not too flat sound. The double row of pipes of the bourdon register . . . definitely the most characteristic one in a street organ . . . can be seen in most organs in the center front, and are easily recognized by the stoppers which close the tops. These stoppers also serve in tuning the pipes. Pulling it slightly upward has the effect of lengthening the air column inside the pipe and the tone becomes lower for the vibration will be slower. Pushing the stopper in has just the opposite effect: the air column becomes shorter, the number of vibrations per second increases, and the sound is higher. From the foregoing, it will be evident that tuning the bourdon flutes is a painstaking job. If one tunes the front flutes too high in comparison to the back ones so that they differ more than six vibrations per second, a sharp, biting sound results instead of the desired rich, throbbing one. Sometimes one hears this disagreeable harsh, biting sound when the sun has been beating down on the front row of bourdon flutes, as a result of which they have warmed up and consequently sound higher than normal.

The bourdon register is preferably used as first or second voice in passages which ought to have a lyrical, sweetly-flowing, sensitive quality. It also lends itself perfectly to playful, frolicsome runs and whimsical trills; in short, to scattering about witty but at the same time, graceful musical jokes. If one should desire to have the bourdon sound extra sentimental in slow passages he can accomplish it in many organs by switching on the "tremolo", which adds a special fluctuating beat to the natural throb of the pipes. Care must be taken not to use it in fast passages, however, for there each note must be clearly distinguishable during the instant it is to play. This would not be the case if the air supply to the pipes should be interrupted by the tremulant at just the precise moment when the pipe was to sound. In other words, if the tremolo were used in fast passages, the result would be a horrible stammering, stuttering sound.

The violin register, which is usually placed in back of the double row of bourdon flutes, is especially suitable for those parts in the music which have to sound forceful and strong. Short and frisky chords can be executed effectively; likewise, fresh and martial-sounding ones may be supplemented harmonically by brief trombone blasts and accentuated rhythmically by percussion.

The range of the notes of the melody register is ordinarily slightly less than two octaves and almost completely chromatic; or rather, that is the case in the scale applied to most organs containing only melody, the so-called "56-key Limonaire scale". Here there are 22 keys reserved for mel-

ody, starting with g in the small octave through f"
(double-lined), and chromatic except for e*b*. In the illustration you can see the complete 56-key Limonaire scale
with all the names of the keys as they are laid out in the
clavier. The top of the scale corresponds with the end of the
clavier farthest inside the organ. Besides the different notes
of the bass, accompaniment, and melody, you will see in
this scale also the keys for the stick of the large drum and
cymbal (they play together), both sticks for the small
drum, both clappers (only in a few organs), the drawing

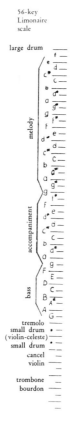

of the stops, and the tremulant. The unused keys are for reserve registers, or, historically speaking, for stops which were sometimes installed in the original Limonaire product but which were discontinued in the period from 1920-1940: vox humana, piccolo, etc.

Even today there are many organs with this 56-key scale, such as the well-known "De Drie Pruiken" (The Three Wigs), "De Brandweer" (The Fire Department, an organ in which there was originally a bell reminiscent of those used by fire departments), "De Klok" (The Bell), "Het Blauwtje" (The Blue), "Het Witje" (The White), "De Schietgaten" (The Shooting Holes, from the openings to the left and right with the drums behind them), "De Buffel" (The Buffalo), "De Limonaire", "Het Zwaantje" (The Swan), "De Omke Romke", and "Het Snotneusje" (The Snotnose).

Those organs with not only melody registers but also some for harmony contain four groups of pipes, three the same as those we have just described and in addition:

The registers for harmony.

The added dimension of organs which contain registers for harmony as well as melody is that it is possible to play a melody of a given tonal color against a counter melody of a completely different quality. One could play a melody in bright melody registers against a counter melody performed on the heavy and melancholy-sounding harmony registers. The process could also be reversed, having the main melody in harmony registers sounding forceful and radiant, with an obligatto of fast and nimble passages on high and ethereal-sounding melody registers. It would take too long to exhaust the innumerable possibilities of the combinations which could be made up by interweaving the various registers in both these groups. We shall return once more to the different kinds of harmony registers when we compare the Belgian organs with those built by Carl Frei. At this time we want to point out that in general the number of keys for harmony varies from approximately 12 to 18 and thus spans one to one and a half octaves. Ordinarily the harmony is about half an octave lower than the melody in the same organ. It does occur, however, that the lowest notes of the melody and the harmony are the same, but that the harmony does not continue as far into the treble. Generally speaking, not only is the tonal span of the harmony lower than that of the melody, but the sound character is also heavier and deeper.

To illustrate what we have been explaining, we are printing here the notation for the beginning of the song, "Why Are You Crying, Little Louise?", as I arranged it for the 90-key Carl Frei organ, "De Negentiger" (The Ninety). More about the disposition of this organ later. The fact that the tune is written in A♭ is due to the transposition upwards of a minor third by the organ. Therefore, according to the scale the music is not written in A♭, but in F. In reality the music plays in A♭, as it is indicated in the example. For each of the four above-mentioned main groups we have used a separate staff. Reading from bottom to top, they are for: the basses, the accompaniment, harmony, and melody. You must imagine that the melody is being executed by bourdon with tremolo, and the harmony by a sentimental and melancholy-sounding cello register (for Louise is crying!). The mournful character of the cello part is made even more "blue" sounding by the chromatic descent of the harmony.

164

We hope that it has not been too difficult for you to follow this explanation of the disposition of the pierement, but
it was necessary if we were effectively to clarify the difference between Belgian and Carl Frei organs.

On, then, to the Belgian organs. Those that were built
with only registers for melody usually followed the above-
outlined disposition (violin and bourdon). As far as these
smaller organs is concerned, the difference from the Carl
Frei organs is not so much in the disposition as in the timbre and volume of the pipes. It is important to bear in
mind, particularly a little later on when we turn our attention to the limpid registers of the Carl Frei organs, that
various Belgian organs from the period 1925-1930 already
possessed beautiful bourdon parts in melody. Remarkably
enough, however, they were all instruments with only melody registers and not those with both harmony and melody!
We think here in particular of the smaller De Vreese organs,
like "De Papagaai" (The Parrot), "De Goudkip" (The
Golden Head), and "De Gaspijp" (The Gaspipe).

The greater part of the Belgian organs, however, were
furnished with different registers for melody and harmony
from the outset. This is to be expected when we remember
that the dance organs in general were also built with a great
many registers for melody and harmony.

165

In the melody section of the Belgian organs there is always a violin register. In some cases a more or less similar register is situated directly behind it, the undamaris, sometimes also called "ondumaris", which means: waves of the sea. This name is descriptive of these open pipes with frein ("brake", or metal plate at the mouth) which usually have double the length of the violin pipes of the corresponding notes of the scale. The undamaris serves primarily to strengthen the violin and is "drawn" together with the violin in the forte passages. As a third melody register we mention the flute harmonique, which was discussed earlier. Fourth is the carillon register which was sometimes found in the Belgian organs, but was later removed in many instances. This stop consists partially of wood and partially of thin metal pipes which are tuned in overtones, namely octave and quint. In some cases, however, the carillon register consists of wood pipes only. The tone, which is high and piercing, gave the stop its name, for it resembles the treble bells of a carillon, in which overtones also play an important part. Actually, the carillon register is only suitable for "waterfalls" and other musical adornments with short notes in quick succession frolicking about above all the other registers. In addition to the registers consisting of pipes, in some Belgian organs, especially those of De Cap and Pierre Verbeeck, there was installed in the melody section a metallophon, consisting of metal plates struck by small hammers.

In the harmony of the Belgian organs the two most common registers are the celeste, consisting of open pipes with frein strongly reminiscent of the violins because of their biting, bowing sound and, in effect, their counterpart, and the cello, consisting of large open pipes with frein which are twice as long and so sound an octave lower than the celeste. In many Belgian organs it is possible to contrast the bowing quality of the celeste and cello registers, which are almost always combined in forceful-sounding passages, with a register of a completely different quality: the meek-sounding bourdon! Nota bene: this bourdon differs markedly in sound character from the above-described bourdon in melody. This one sounds much softer and is much less assertive, due to the way in which the pipes are voiced. Like the bourdon in melody, it is tuned with a slight dissonance to achieve the characteristic beat: this is the essential and indispensable quality of the bourdon register! Another hollow and soft-sounding register, which has fallen into disuse, is the flute 8, primarily used for fast-flowing passages. In the larger Belgian pierements we also frequently encounter the baritone in the harmony section. It consists of fairly wide, open pipes, two to a note, one of which is supplied with a reed. The other serves to compensate somewhat for the blatant sound of the reed, and to strengthen the dark and sonorous quality of the register.

We shall now define the important differences between the Carl Frei and the Belgian organs as they existed before the Belgian builders began to follow in Frei's footsteps. In making this comparison, our first premise will be that the latter paid more heed to the quality than to the quantity of his registers, for the Belgian instruments usually have larger numbers of them than his do, in spite of which the Frei organs as a rule are superior in volume of sound. Another difference . . . and this is the most important one . . . is that the sound character of Frei's instruments is much clearer and more transparent than that of the Belgian product, principally the result of his voicing of the pipes. With the smaller organs, which had only registers for melody, he followed the 56-key Limonaire scale, building in the bourdon and violin registers as we have mentioned above. When it comes to the larger instruments with both melody and harmony, the differences are even greater. For one thing, the division of the registers was completely different, one of the most striking being the placing of the bourdon. As we have seen in the Belgian organs, this stop is found in harmony with a rather soft, muted quality, but generally not in melody. In contrast, Carl Frei gave it a prominent position in melody (with clear, pronounced voicing), and did not use it in harmony.

Concerning the harmony in Carl Frei organs, we must first point out the "specialty of the house", featured in all his instruments with a harmony section: namely, the undamaris. Here again we find a pronounced contrast with the Belgian organs, in which this stop was included in the melody but not the harmony. Even more significant is the fact that the Frei undamaris had a much fuller, warmer, and more radiant sound. The pipes he built for this stop were extraordinarily wide. In his arrangements he sometimes used the undamaris in single-voiced harmony along with the accompaniment, but frequently used it in complete chords, which formed a warm and harmonious background for the melody of the bourdon or the violins.

The Frei instruments with melody and harmony both can be separated into two main groups: the 72-key and the 90-key organs. The scale of the 72-key organs consists of the traditional 56-key Limonaire scale, with the addition of 13 keys for harmony, from g through g' (thus one completely chromatic octave) and three keys for registers and tremolo in harmony. Several of these 72-key organs are rebuilt Belgian instruments, mostly De Cap, which derived their names from the figures originally painted on the side panels which were removed during the rebuilding and re-

---

Example of the type of street organ current about 1930 with the painted side panels replaced by open carved work. Although the flower girl has been replaced by a flower basket, the organ has kept its original name.

placed by open carving. In this way the man with the goatee in the organ "De Sik" (The Goatee) was replaced by carving including a squirrel. Although the owner of the instrument, the well-known agent Willem van Jaaren, re-christened it "De Eekhoorn" (The Squirrel), it is still known by its old name in the organ world. Could it be this feeling of faithfulness to a once-given name to which we owe the fact that in a similarly-rebuilt 72-key organ, "De Duif" (The Dove), with side panels portraying a lady with a dove, a dove was carved into the open work designed to replace these paintings? And that in the organ, "De Bloemenmeid" (The Flower Girl) the side panels were re-placed by carving featuring, not a flower girl, but a flower basket? The reason why the side panels were replaced by carving was that in this way the registers Frei built into the side cases could be heard to better advantage, and from the front of the organ. One of these cases contained the har-mony registers, and the other, an extra register for melody. This was the celeste, which practically always played in combination with the violins and was primarily intended as reinforcement for that stop. The sound quality of this celeste was fresh and keen and it was always used in melody, also in contrast to the Belgian instruments where it was used in harmony. Another step forward was that Frei usu-ally had the complete stop in each side case and did not, therefore, follow the Belgian practice of dividing into a right and a left half, which better conserved the musical coherence of the registers involved.

In the case of the 72-key style, Frei limited himself in most organs to the usual disposition: violin, celeste, and bourdon in melody and undamaris in harmony, notably in "De Sik", "De Duif", "De Twee Rozen" (The Two Roses), "De Stolwijker", "De Gavioli", and the unforgettable, un-fortunately no-longer-in-service "Tiet" (Tit). In some instances he added another quite remarkable register, the biphone (Greek for "double sound") to both the melody and the harmony. This stop has two stopped pipes playing for each key, ordinarily, of 16-foot pitch, or twice as long as the bourdon. When in melody sometimes only one rank of stopped pipes, also 16-foot, plays, but then in combination with the violin and no celeste. In both melody and harmony the sound character of the biphone is fairly soft and mysterious, with a rather nasal quality in melody and a deep, hollow sound in harmony. This mysterious character is emphasized by the regular use of the tremulant. Examples of 72-key organs with biphone are "De Bloemenmeid" and "De Puntkap" (The Pointed Cap.)

While the biphone is rather rare in 72-key organs, in the 90-key style it came into regular use as biphone I for melody and biphone II for harmony. The 90-key scale contained: 22 keys for melody (the same as in the 56 and 72-key instruments), 18 keys for harmony (in comparison with the 72-key scale, an expansion into the treble of 5 notes, for a total of an octave and a half: from g through c"), and 17 for accompaniment (an extension downwards to include g♯, f♯, f, e, and c.)

The first 90-key organ appeared on the street in 1930, the famous "Negentiger" (Ninety). It is still considered by many to be the finest street organ Carl Frei built. It differs from most other 90-key organs in having a beautiful, warm cello in harmony. The pipes of this register are not supplied with the "frein", or harmonic brake, so that the quality is not of "bowing" but is rather dark and melancholy in character. As we have said, the cello was not built into most of the 90-key organs, so that the disposition was as follows: violin, celeste, bourdon and biphone I for melody, and undamaris and biphone II for harmony. Some organs which were built or rebuilt according to this dis-

The 90-key Carl Frei organ "The Golden One" now at Leeuwarden. On the lower front center is a painting of "De Oldehove".

position are, "De Bifoon" (The Biphone), "De Hindenburg", "De Pod" (see page 178), "De Blauwe Pilaar" (The
Blue Pillar), "De Cementmolen" (The Cement Mill), and
"De Gouwe" (The Golden One). This last was the last one
Frei turned out, and in our opinion was also the most
beautiful. It was finished in 1938 after a complete rebuilding, necessary because most of it burned in a cafe in Zaandam (near Amsterdam). Originally it was a Pierre Verbeeck instrument. The special appeal of this opus of Frei's
is at least partly due to the peculiar timbre of the biphone
II, which features one rank of pipes tuned an octave higher
than the other (thus 8 and 16-foot).

However happy we might be to give more particulars
about the Frei products, it is time to go on now to the next
subject. Please forgive us if we do not elaborate on the
organs originally built for dance halls but later used in the
streets, the "Zaalorgel" (Hall Organ), the two "Radiokasten" (Radio Cases) with the distinctive feature of half-
closed "radio flutes" in melody, and above all, the famous
"Harmonica", the 90-key organ with an accordion built in
and alternating with the other registers, supported by the
ground basses and the undamaris.

Finally we want to point out that the Frei organs became
so famous that they were imitated more and more. For example, the bourdon in melody was so generally appreciated
by renters and listeners alike that in many organs which
never had a bourdon room was made to install one by removing another register such as flute harmonique or carillon. This was done, for instance in "De Arabier", "De
Mondorgel", and the "70 Burssens". It is interesting that,
due to the fact the original bourdon in harmony was maintained, one can now clearly distinguish the difference in
tone between these two bourdons. The new Belgian organs
began to bear a strong resemblance to Frei's work during

the last years prior to the second World War. The most striking examples are the 67-key instruments of Burssens, "De Vier Jaargetijden" (The Four Seasons) and the "IJzeren Hein" (Iron Henry). In these organs also the disposition was violin and bourdon for melody with undamaris for harmony. Because the pipes of the undamaris registers in these Burssens organs were much smaller and the sound, therefore, was much more restrained, we cannot say that these instruments equalled Frei's, at least not as far as the harmony is concerned!

The Street Organ Domain in the Twenties and the Thirties

Between the first and second World Wars Amsterdam remained Holland's "first city" regarding street organs. This was in no way changed by the spectacular and sensational auction November 23, 1923, of the pierements which had belonged to the brothers Leon and Gabriel Warnies, occasioned by the liquidation of the firm because of family circumstances including the death of Gabriel. A colorful mixture of organs harking back to different periods in the history of the firm and all standing together could be viewed. In browsing about one could admire new Belgian organs, such as the "Tubantia" and the "Carillon" (both 64-key Burssens) as well as older French book organs like the "Turk" (62-key Limonaire), the "Kleine Buik" (Little Belly), and the "Tambourijn" (Tambourine), both 56-key Limonaire, and many Gasparini's. But there were still some cylinder organs surviving from father Leon's time. It was a spectacle which could not help but impress others than those specifically interested in organs. Johann Luger wrote of his impressions in "Het Leven" (Life) of Saturday, December 1, 1923:

"Borstplaat (a brightly-colored candy popular around St. Nicolas . . . Dec. 5 . . . and Christmas) lit up by a

174

heavenly sunset . . . blue and poisonous copper-green . . . banana yellow and luncheon-meat pink . . . all the pastel colors of all the sweaters on all tennis courts. And the dolls! (the animated carved figures) This is how the people on Goudsbloemdwarsstraat (Marigold Drive) picture the characters in tales of knights and chivalry: pages and beautiful maidens, their noble faces covered with the sugary red of cheap rouge . . . a pat on the cheeks and some on the lips. There is no designer nor craftsman living who could dream up such a mixed-up, riotous Baroque as this. The macaroni starts to writhe at the foot of the organ, changes into Krakeling (a pretzel-shaped sweet cookie) part way up, and winds up at the peak in an exotic flourish of colorful, graceful sprays. They are just exquisite, that is all one can say."

To be candid, we must add that Luger had a less favorable opinion of the early cylinder organs: "Those small, sneaky organs, which look like nothing so much as a suitcase on top of a pushcart. These camouflaged sneaks slink unobserved into the midst of the hustle and bustle, and then suddenly, without warning, burst into such a sentimental, mournful outpouring that stray dogs lose their carefree mien and slink away, their tails between their legs. They are the worst and . . . the dearest, used by the outcasts of the trade, those who know nothing of the stately tempi of the masters. They earn their living on pity rather than the well-earned proceeds of an honorable service performed. They have no following of enthusiastic admirers to serve as guardians on the public roads and teach the howling dogs a few manners by a well-placed kick; they are the poorest of the poor, who bring upon the human soul a melancholy to make one shiver." Author Luger, who is a non-initiate into the organ world, hereby only confirms what we have already written in chapter 8 about the difference between cylinder and book system organs.

Startled, and not without concern, you will be wondering what the outcome of such a public sale of pierements must have been. Would the instruments be saved? Or might they not fall into the hands of the wrong buyers and thus be lost forever? Would it indeed become "The Black Day of the Organ World", as the title of the above-mentioned article in "Het Leven" read? Happily, the answer is a resounding "no!" Practically all the organs auctioned off remained in the family. What happened? Old Leon Warnies had, besides the sons Leon and Gabriel, whom we have already mentioned, several daughters. One, Susanna, had married a man named Mohlmann, deceased at the time of the auction, by whom she had a son, Henk, now 21 years old. Another daughter, Leontine Ermina, was married to G. Perlee, who had started his own rental agency in 1910. A significant portion of the instruments came into possession of the widow Mohlmann-Warnies. She bought the fourteen best organs, including those mentioned above. Some others were bought by G. Perlee and were used in his firm, which operated under the name Perlee-Warnies. Thus, what Luger had predicted in connection with the auction in Frascati Hall came about: "But the dogs will resume barking when this caravan continues on its way again after a short rest, passing the closed-up house fronts, bombarding the windows with music which evokes the sunshine of other lands: for Warnies does not die . . . Warnies is dead . . . vive Warnies!" The direct descendents of Warnies are still the ones who set the pace in the organ world.

In the years after this notorious auction, more and more Carl Frei organs made their debut alongside the old French and the new Belgian ones. At first, this took place, as far as Amsterdam was concerned, only in the firm of Mohlmann-

Warnies ("Schietgaten", both "Radiokasten", "Cello", "Snuffeltje" (Snoopy), etc.) but after 1933 also in the stock of Willem van Jaaren on Vinkenstraat, another rental agent which had been established in the meantime.

Van Jaaren was a very important man in the business between 1930 and 1942. It was he who took over most of the stock of the Nuberg concern, mostly Belgian organs and particularly those of De Cap, with oriental and other beauties painted on their side panels. Van Jaaren got things off to a flying start and had many instruments rebuilt by Carl Frei, for which, fortunately, he had the necessary funds. We have already described how at the time of the restoration of these organs, the side panels were replaced by carved open work. To avoid misunderstanding, we want to make it clear that Carl Frei did not do this work, but rather it was accomplished in the shop of Van Jaaren. While Frei built new registers in the cases, the wood carver Gijs van Nieuwkerk did the restorations and alterations of the facades. He was the man who did the doves, the squirrels, and the flowerbaskets. Thus, because of the initiative of Willem van Jaaren, the technical knowledge of Carl Frei, and the artistry of "Uncle Gijs, the Carver", the rebuilding of the following instruments was effected: "Tiet", "Sik", "Duif", "Bloemenmeid", and "Gavioli" (all 72-key); and "Blauwe Pilaar", "Pod", and "Cement-molen" (all 90-key). To this list was added in 1938 "De Gouwe" (90-key), the last one to be done.

I shall not easily forget how I made it a special point at that time (my secondary school years) to see to it that all these new organs were alternately rented out for a period of six months to a licensee in Groningen, Mother Helmes, a charming woman whom I considered more or less my second mother. At that time there were two licensees in Groningen, one of whom had bought his own De Vreese organ at the beginning of the thirties and had kept on the Groningen streets until in 1942 the Germans forbade all street organs in general. For rental of Van Jaaren's instruments, only Mother Helmes was considered. She had a team of three men to do the actual working of the organs: her son, her brother, and a boarder. The first was, although by far the youngest, the "boss". It was not at all easy to get the best organs for Groningen again and again, for at that time also the older Amsterdam licensees had preference because of seniority. But Van Jaaren also had a soft spot in his heart for Mother Helmes ... possibly because, in contrast to the Amsterdam people, she always paid faithfully, even on rainy days. In Amsterdam they make it a habit not to go out with the organs in bad weather. Instead, they remain in the halls of the agent on those days, and many of the organ grinders congregate there too, so that you can hear all kinds of interesting and strong stories. But ... such days are deducted from the rent! Not so in Groningen ... there they went out on rainy days too. The organs were covered three quarters of the way with canvas, the back completely except for an access flap near the mechanical part, and the front so far that no rain could get into the pipes. The zenith of the career of Mother Helmes and her men (I had the audacity to consider myself "fourth man") came when we succeeded in bringing the organ "De Pod" to Groningen. I later heard that this instrument had acquired its name in Amsterdam because Jan de Pod used it for several years. Van Jaaren called it "De Mooie Kap" (The Beautiful Top). We were able to get it to Gronginen because I added fl. 1.50 weekly to the organ rent from my allowance. The standard rent was fl. 15.00 weekly, but "De Pod", as an elite instrument, had to bring in fl. 16.50. I did not want to force Mother Helmes to pay more than the normal price, because she rented it for my sake. It never entered my mind to try to subtract fl. 1.50 a week, say for rainy days, for I considered van Jaaren the king of the organ world and looked up to him enormously. On one occasion I had to act as his host in Groningen, and I took him to dinner at the Doelen hotel, the best in town. I would have been better off to take him to an establishment where the menu was less sophisticated but more substantial, for his size bore witness to a hearty appetite. When I hear someone speak of the organ "De grote Buik" (Big Belly), I always have to think of "Uncle Willem", although I would not have dared call him "Uncle" at that time, of course. The witticisms which he aired during the course of the meal were not really appropriate for the Doelen Hotel. When the hare was being served, he uttered a pained "meaow", and when I asked him to help himself to the applesauce, he answered laconically, "Thank you, but I won't be doing any wallpapering right now." But, just the same we had a lot of fun together. How we laughed once when he was at Mother Helme's house and he suddenly got up and started singing in a solemn voice to the tune of our national anthem: "Will Helmes, bring me a drink . . ." (The verse actually starts with the word "Wilhelmus", the name of William of Orange.) It was too bad that he sold all his organs after 1942 and did not begin again after the war. He died on September 2, 1959 at the age of 82.

Unfortunately, we cannot elaborate as much on all the rental agents as we have on Willem van Jaaren, but will content ourselves with the mention of the names of Piet Bik, Amsterdam, and Piet Winter, Zaandam. In the second street organ city, Rotterdam, Timmermans and Diepstraten conducted business, in addition to Louis Holvoet and Goudswaard, whom we have already mentioned. While Timmermans imported instruments from Belgium exclusively, mainly built by De Cap, Holvoet, and Goudswaard,

Diepstraten bought mostly from Carl Frei. Holvoet introduced in 1930 the famous "Negentiger" in Rotterdam, a trump card over Amsterdam! Diepstraten was very successful with the Frei organ "Het Zaalorgel", which he bought from the Lekkerkerk (a small town near Rotterdam) rental agent G. van der Wouden, incidentally one of the first to use Frei instruments. It was a black day for Rotterdam when fire broke out in Timmerman's hall and many of the organs were lost.

But how about the other large cities; were there no organ renters to be found there? Only in one! In The Hague there was the firm of Theo Denies on Nieuwe Havenstraat. From the fact that he had as a goal the possession of one hundred organs it is evident that he was a significant figure in the development of the pierement in the thirties. He did not quite reach that figure, but he did manage forty-seven, which is a quite respectable number. Denies in particular imported Belgian organs, mostly from Burssens, during the period when they were being built more and more in the style of Carl Frei both inwardly and outwardly. Some of the well-known Denies instruments were: "De Zaza", "De Bioscoopfluit" (The Movie Flute), "De Mondorgel" (The Mouthorgan), "De IJseren Hein", and "De Vier Jaargetijden". It is interesting to note that even today many organs which belonged to Denies can be recognized by the disposition, unless they have been rebuilt, for in the Denies organs generally no trombones were to be found. He thought they went out of tune too easily ... which is only too true! He simply omitted the register, and in place of it had the ground basses strengthened by upper basses.

Those readers who are particularly interested in dramatic happenings will be interested to hear that in 1929 "De Zaza" was split in two by a trolley car in The Hague. From legal records it appears that after a long suit during which

180

Denies requested restitution under article 1403 of the applicable law of the city, he won.

The atmosphere around the organs is of course, largely a reflection of the exploiters proper; that is to say, those who rent and play the instruments. (Only rarely does it happen that the grinder is also the owner of the instrument with which he makes a living for himself, his family, and also the families of his helpers.) The licensee, or the one to whom the city government gives permission "to make music on the public streets by way of a street organ" is usually the renter. Sometimes this renter-licensee employs two men, one with whom he works in partnership, and a third whom they hire to do the grinding while they act as "mansers" (collectors of money). The licensees are often recruited from men who have shown their ability as helpers of other licensees. Many times the job is passed on from father to son, and it sometimes happens that various members of one family are engaged in working different organs. Then a so-called "dynasty" of organ players is created. One well-known example is the Amsterdam family Lurks. Father Lurks, known as "ome Dolf" (Uncle Dolf), had already been a well-known figure in the organ world before the war, and was the oldest licensee there was afterwards. The many confidential talks I had with him always began with his expression; "Over u gezegd . . ." ("Talking about you . . .") when what he meant to say was, "Onder ons gezegd . . ." ("Just between you and me . . ."). The spouse of "ome Dolf" is "tante Anne", who collaborates with another licensee, Manus Hotman, nicknamed "Ezeltje" (Donkey). Her son, Akkie Lurks, also has a license and has had Roeltje Schutte as a permanent partner for years. The latter has acquired the nickname "De Duikboot" (Submarine) because he threatens to dive forward when he holds out the moneybox to the passersby in a friendly way.

Both the grinding and the collecting of the money are arts in themselves. To turn the heavy wheel one has to have great physical endurance and, preferably, a good sense of rhythm, or rather style. I invite you to play one of the organs all the way through a book. I am sure you will find it difficult to maintain the right tempo with no variations, and that you will be completely out of breath at the end. An organgrinder, however, has to keep it up from 8:00 a.m. to 8:00 p.m., or in winter, half an hour after sundown. Fortunately, practice has shown that most organgrinders do their work not only with devotion to duty, but also with enjoyment. And this is where an important principle applies! It is not enough just to give it a turn, you have to like it yourself to be able to give it the right swing! Can a grinder possess a special aptitude through which he can distinguish himself from the run-of-the-mill; that is, become a specialist? Certainly! When this comes about, he earns the appellation "stijldraaier" (style-turner). The ordinary, good grinder, who has no aspirations to specialize as a "style-turner", will play the book through in one and the same tempo. In this case the music will sound beautiful, if it has been arranged correctly, because the arranger has already taken care of all changes and shadings of tempo, assuming that the book would be played through at the same rate of speed; to wit, about five centimeters per second. However, where romantic works are concerned, in which varying tempi, accelerandos, ritenutos, fermatas, and general pauses are effective, the operator can emphasize the interpretation of the composer and the adaptor. He can do this by increasing the speed in fast parts and slackening off in others (taking care, of course, not to slow down too much or the bellows would collapse and the air would consequently only sigh instead of blow), and by momentarily stopping or even letting go completely for a second at the general pauses. Then the music is executed in "tempo rubato", the extent of which is determined by the personal taste of the player. The romantic character of this type of music can stand it!

For collecting the money (mansen) other qualities are required. Maybe it is asking too much to expect that the collectors bring the listeners under a kind of hypnosis... as the pierement itself can do so well! But at least he has to be a good psychologist. He must, while ambling amiably about, notice immediately whether a flash in the eyes of the passersby betrays a real love (or passion?) for the pierement, even though it may be unconscious, or suppressed by a false sense of pride.

The musicians must also know how to divide a city into sections, distinguishing between the residential sections, the commercial sections of stores, etc., and the so-called "permanent stand". This last is definitely the most lucrative work, but the collector must be experienced and have a great deal of psychological insight. The organ in this case remains for a long time in a spot where many people pass by. While one book after another is played, the collectors have to extract as much as possible from the passers-by, being very polite and knowing just how far to go with their joking. They have to avoid anything which smacks of forcing a donation from the public. They should execute the movements with the boxes in time with the music and with graceful motions. The boxes should never be pointed at the pedestrians like a gun!

In concluding this chapter, we want to try to convey a little of the flavor of life around street organs in Amsterdam during this period. People habitually couple the pierement with the "Jordaan" (a famous section of Amsterdam), and not without reason, because the important organ renters have always lived and plied their trade there, on streets like Brouwersgracht, Westerstraat, Haarlemmer-houttuinen, Vinkenstraat, etc. Gijs Perlee and Henk Mohlmann still have their firm in the Jordaan, which was indeed a beloved section between 1920 and 1940. It is not quite the same now! I remember how several organs belonging to Van Jaaren used to meet on the Lindengracht on Saturday afternoons about 1937 to 1939. I had arranged my first organ book and punched it out in Van Jaaren's shop (a potpourri from Walt Disney's cartoon "Snow White"), and I had the opportunity to try it out successively on "De Tiet", "De Gavioli", and "De Bloemenmeid" on the Lindengracht, although it was meant for "De Sik" alias "De Eekhoorn" in Groningen.

The one thing which stands out most vividly in my mind about the people involved with the pierements of that time is that they were all so spontaneous, jovial, and warm-hearted, with a great sense of humor and above all a deep love for their instruments. They treated them as if they were human beings, busying themselves with the organs even on Sunday, when they cleaned them thoroughly. One could have very decent talks about the organ repertory with them, for they often showed a healthy inborn musical sense. To be sure, their terminology did differ somewhat from ours. Where we would say "romantic", they would say "it makes you cry". If we wanted to make clear to them that we thought a book was "harmonically correct and well arranged", they would sum it up: "Yes, it runs just right." If someone was praised because of his penetrating psychological insight, they would agree to it in the following words: "Yes, he has a way with people." One thing that should not be expected is correct pronunciation of the titles of the pieces. There is a well-known story about an organ man who asked for a book, the title of which he had forgotten. He only remembered that it dealt with a man "who had to work hard for his living". Finally the name came back to him, and he said, "I remember now, it's the Overtime of William Tell!" In the case of the well-known French song, "Chante encore dans la Nuit", the title emerges as "Tante Cor van ome Louis" (Auntie Cor of Uncle Louis), and "C'est si bon" becomes "Spersibon" (Green Bean). One should also not be taken off guard at hearing the "Calif of Bagdad" become a "Calf"!

But, enough joking, we must return to developments in Amsterdam. Unfortunately, we must report the fact, at the conclusion of our survey of the period 1920-1940, that after 1935 a change began to be felt in Amsterdam. In the years from 1916-1935 about thirty to thirty-three licences were granted annually, but after 1935 the number dropped as licences of musicians who discontinued their occupation were not issued to others who were interested. The zenith of the pierement was past! The number of officially-playing pierements dwindled from thirty in 1935 to fifteen in 1940. We say "officially", because the deliberate manner in which the city council limited the number of licences led to the fact that more and more disappointed but determined organ people went out with an organ without permission, that is, "took a chance". A silent battle had begun between the city authorities and the organ players. Silent? Nay! The beginning of this battle was far from it! The gauntlet was thrown down when a prohibition was issued against the playing of organs on the Amsterdam "grachten" (the streets lining the canals). This they certainly would not take lying down, and as a protest all the licencees went to the city hall with their organs. Anyone who tries to take the bread and butter out of an organ man's mouth can expect thundering music. I don't blame them! For the Amsterdam "grachten" became famous the world over partially because of the pierement, which was synonymous with them. It has been noted in other cases that such a dramatic occurrence very often does have an inspiring effect on creative artists. Who among you has not heard the plaintive song, "Als van d'Amsterdamse grachten het pierement verdwijnt" (If the Pierement Should Vanish from the Grachten of Amsterdam)?

Alas, the next blow was to be another serious setback for the licencees and a victory for the city council, for soon another ordinance was passed, this time making it illegal for the organs to play anywhere at all in the heart of Amsterdam.

The Notation of the Organ Books

10

Now that we have arrived at the period 1940-1945 in our historical survey, we shall have a fine opportunity to describe the arranging of organ books. During this time there was a hiatus in our story of the pierement because of the occupation and the accompanying prohibition of street organ music, so we are going to put the pause to good use in this way. How often we have been asked to tell "just a little bit" about this art. Unfortunately, we have always had to give the disappointing answer that it is impossible to give a clear picture of the process in one discussion. To understand it, one has to understand the disposition of the various ranks of pipes and how they were intended to be used, and also one must have the chance to study the related illustrations at length. We now assume that our readers possess the former knowledge in "optima forma" ... if necessary, re-read pages 157-171 in chapter 9 ... and as for illustrative material, you will find plenty of it in this book. It is for just this reason that we find it very tempting to capitalize on this opportunity and answer as well as possible all those who ask these questions, and anyone else who may be interested.

Whoever expects us to begin immediately with the "arranging board" and to show the pattern behind the bewildering swarm of holes in an organ book is going to have to be patient for a while, for a purely mental and much more important job has to precede the actual perforation of the music. This could perhaps best be described as "evolving a mental concept of the arrangement". Anyone who can do this can also learn the technique of the actual musical notation, although the opposite is not true: a composer who cannot write down what he creates can always learn to do this. The essential thing is that he hear it in his mind, or soul if you will. On the contrary, not everyone who is capable of taking down musical notation is able to compose it.

You will understand now why we devote our attention first and foremost to the art of arranging music and all that is connected with it before we even consider writing down one note of our tune.

An arranger of organ music will have to have the following capacities:

1. He must have a thorough knowledge of harmony and counterpoint. In this respect he must be the equal of an arranger of orchestral music.

2. He must be creative. In a certain sense, he will have to have the capabilities of a composer, since his task is to arrange a given piece of music correctly regarding harmony, counterpoint, and instrumentation. He will have to follow his own ideas, and develop them himself. For instance, he may have to create a counter-melody to play in the harmony section against the melody line. This is indispensable in street organ music. To put the whole thing simply, an organ is comparable to an orchestra in every respect, as you may have perceived for yourself from our explanation of the disposition.

3. Furthermore, he must be thoroughly acquainted with the musical possibilities of the organ for which he is arranging the music. The most accomplished arranger of orchestral music will be entirely unable to arrange street organ books if he has not previously puzzled out the secrets of the pierement. Do you remember what we wrote at the end of chapter 7 about the many surprising effects which are to be had from a good arrangement? Of course, you

will now be asking us what must be done in order to master this art. Provided you have the required proficiency in harmony and counterpoint and possess the essential creativity, the answer is simple . . . simple, at least, if you have a real love for the pierement, for it is on this one specific element that your success as an arranger or adaptor depends. What you must do is simply to listen often and intently to different kinds of street organs and at last, to pick out one of the many for which you want to arrange some music. Do not choose one with a complicated scale, or with too many registers. Rather, start preferably with a 56-key instrument. Absorb its music. Listen as often and as long as you possibly can, so that eventually you can hear the music in your mind, even when the organ is not playing. At this point, begin imagining it is playing a new tune which you have never actually heard it perform. When you can do this, the next . . . and most important . . . step is: to learn to analyze the music, as you heard it in reality and in your imagination, so that you know how it is put 'together. What it boils down to is distinguishing between the basses, accompaniment, melody, and (if present) harmony; the notes which you hear in these main groups, and the sound quality of the different registers and the combinations thereof. To accomplish this you will have to begin by studying the scale at your leisure to familiarize yourself with the way the three or four main groups and the notes of each one relate to the perforations of the book. Next, watch a book while it is playing so that you can connect the pattern of holes as they disappear under the top section of the clavier with the music you hear a fraction of a second later. Perhaps you will not be able to make this mental association the first time. Don't worry! You can play the same book on the same organ as often as you want . . . a more patient teacher than a street organ does not exist. When you have trained yourself this way, you should take the books home and re-read them at your leisure. A cardboard strip with the scale on it can be a big help at this time, for you can move it along the music as you read and in this way identify the perforations, whether they be for notes, registers, cancel, percussion, baton, or what. When you have mastered this, you should also try to read a book that you have not heard play, and, finally, to analyze music which has not even been made into a book. At this point the time is ripe to try your hand at your first arrangement.

After this comprehensive introduction we can afford to be fairly concise about the way in which the arranger puts his adaptation together. First he has to determine what key will do the arrangement the most justice, which is mainly dependent on the range of the melody and harmony sections, and the number of basses available to him. Then he can harmonize the music, including variations in the melody, correct chords in basses and accompaniment, and, if present, a counter-melody in the harmony section. He also will have to lay out the proper registration to make the final effect as translucent and clear as possible, and accent it here and there with percussion. Moreover, it will also be necessary to devise preludes, interludes, and postludes and weave them into the arrangement. Of course, one can avail himself of a piano, harmonium, or accordion, but these instruments remain fairly limited means of help, usually, for the registration cannot be reproduced and in most cases the melody, harmony, basses, and accompaniment cannot be played simultaneously. Of course, the arranger can write his adaptation down in ordinary music notation, or make other notes about his conception of it. When all of this has taken place, the arranger must be able to hear the whole

---

Carl Frei at the arranging barrel.

190

thing in his mind. When the instrument performs it for the first time, he will have the feeling that he has heard it play before, and it could be that he suddenly says to himself: "That is the way it should be; so far I have heard it only in my imagination but now I hear it in reality."

Before going on to the discussion of the actual technique of perforation, we want to make the following observations: we have just made a distinction between the "development of the concept" of the arrangement and the actual notation, not only to point out the difference between the two, but principally so that the arranger will not start trying to punch out music without having the arrangement clearly in his mind and knowing what effect he is trying to achieve. Actually, this is no different from setting down conventional musical arrangements on staff paper. It does happen sometimes, of course, that the arranger develops the work right at the arranging board, but when a work is commissioned on short notice this cannot be helped.

The notation proper is done on a board or barrel. While Carl Frei used to use a barrel, nowadays the Dutch use a board. Due to the abridged character of this chapter, we can discuss only one of the two methods at length, so we have chosen the board since it is the more common. The objects and materials needed are a board which is supplied

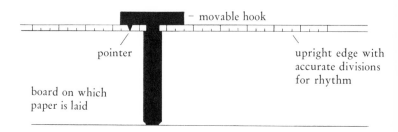

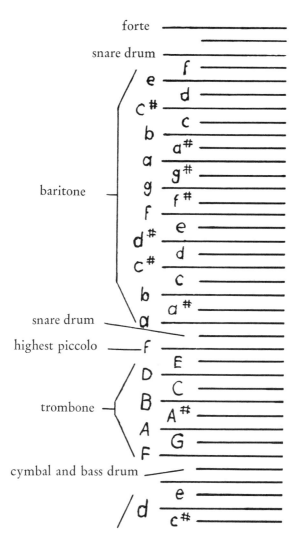

with one upright edge which is perfectly straight; a T-shaped hook which can be placed on top of the board and moved along it as indicated in the illustration (we shall mention the pointer on this hook later on), a roll of paper, a pencil or ball point pen and . . . last but not least . . . the scale of the organ for which the music is being done.

This is usually on a long piece of cardboard. It could be on a thin board, but a strip of organ-book cardboard is easily available to an arranger and it does the job perfectly. The names of the keys of the organ involved are marked on it in the correct order of succession, and the length of the strip should correspond with the width of the book. It is recommended that a punch mark be made in the cardboard for each key, so that the edge is notched. The distance between the notches should be the same as the distance between the keys of the clavier. While on this subject, let us note that in book organs with key claviers, the distance between the keys is uniform, and they are spaced so that for every 6 centimeters there are approximately seventeen keys. To clarify this, you have only to look at the preceding illustration (life size) of the top section of the same scale (89-key Gavioli) which is provided in the foldout inside the back cover of this book at two-fifths of life size.

The arranger proceeds as follows: he rolls out the paper and puts it on top of the board, taking care to match the top edge evenly with the upright strip at the top of the board. At the ends of the board he puts weights to keep the paper from sliding. It can also be taped down. It is on this paper that the music has to be marked. The first thing to do is to divide for rhythm, an operation which is accomplished with the aid of the T-shaped hook. These divisions must be indicated clearly by vertical lines on the upper surface of the upright piece attached to the arranging board. The more frequent divisions (consisting of multiples of $\frac{1}{2}$ centimeter) can be marked permanently on the wood; others will have to be made on narrow strips of paper the same width as the upright piece and fastened to it as needed. Now the arranger puts the hook in position over the edge till the pointer is exactly in line with the bar with which he wants to begin and draws a vertical line on the paper along the hook. Then he slides the hook over so that the pointer indicates the next bar and draws another vertical line, etc. When all the bar lines have been drawn in this way, the measures thus produced are numbered. You will still have to know how far apart these bars have to be drawn. To this end, first we will have to premise that the speed of the book through the clavier is approximately 5 centimeters per second. For a fast waltz measure which lasts approximately one second, about 5 centimeters would therefore be needed. Because a waltz is written in 3/4 time, this distance would then have to be subdivided into three equal parts, meaning that the lines indicating the beats of a fast waltz would be $16\frac{2}{3}$ millimeters apart. The 4/4 measure of a tango takes 2 seconds, so that a measure takes up a total of 10 centimeters and the four beats will be $2\frac{1}{2}$ cm apart. The 4/4 measure of a slow foxtrot contains 8 cm so that a line will have to be drawn every 2 cm for the beats. When one is arranging a march, 6 cm will be required and each beat will take $1\frac{1}{2}$ cm if the time is 4/4, while each beat will require exactly 1 cm if the march is in 6/8 time.

When the lines have been drawn and the measures numbered, the actual notation begins. This is done with the help of the scale, the top slid along the upright edge of the arranging board. By putting the tip of the pencil or ball point pen in the notch of the desired note and sliding the hook along for the length of the note, one marks it down as a horizontal line on the paper. After what we have told you about dividing measures and beats, it goes without saying that with a march in 4/4 time a note of one beat is $1\frac{1}{2}$ cm long, a note of two beats 3 cm, and a note of 4 beats 6 cm. However, in march tempo when one has to have short, powerful chords sounded in staccato rather than legato, the perforations cannot last a whole beat but will have to be cut off with only half, or 8 mm. This also goes for the

chords in the accompaniment, for they serve only to accompany rhythmically and so cannot be too drawn out. As
it happens, they usually amount to 7, 8, or 9 mm depending
on the time signature involved.

When a melody must be executed legato, one can have
the notes flow into each other by drawing each one out a
few millimeters past the beginning of the next one. Similarly, one can also overlap the notes of a glissando (popularly called "waterfall"). A few illustrations follow to car-
ify, with standard music notation above and notation for
the same thing in an organ book below.

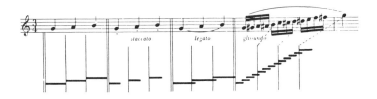

Not only the notes themselves, but also register changes,
percussion, and even the movements of the conductor's
baton are similarly noted with horizontal lines. As far as
percussion is concerned, one has to take into consideration
that the drumsticks have to be beaten against the drum in a
fast tempo and immediately afterwards, must fall back.
For the snare drum the lines are drawn not longer than 6
mm per stroke, while for the heavier, somewhat slower beat
of the bass drum with cymbal, usually 8 mm is used. The
lines for the conductor are marked in the second half of the
measure, resulting in the rise of the arm in the second half
of the measure and the fall exactly on the first beat of the
next measure, so that the conductor indicates the first note
of each new measure.

Finally, we must describe a process for achieving a tremolo effect. This is done simply by writing one long held

note as a number of short lines, usually amounting to about 6 mm in length, with about 2 or 3 mm in between each time. This system is often employed when one wants to have a slow melody play in octaves in the violin register but still avoid the somewhat tight effect resulting from such a unison. The low notes are written normally and the high ones with the short interruptions just described.

Utilizing the various principles and techniques just outlined, the arranger now has to put down on paper as if by magic all the basses, accompaniments, melodies, harmonies, trills, ornaments, drums, castanets, register changes, and movements of the carved figures as they have been conceived by him in advance. Whenever the paper on the board has been filled, it is shifted over to provide a new blank section, and the next section of the music is marked on it, and so on until the final chord is reached. (See what is said about repeats on page 200.)

The critical reader will be wondering: "But why write all this on paper? Why not put the cardboard book itself on the arranging board right away?" In principle this is entirely possible and it is being done. However, there are several advantages to using paper first that will speak for themselves as we proceed with the punching out of the books. This is done with a punching machine which consists . . . if the contrary is not expressly stated . . . of the following steel parts:

1. The punch table on which the book rests during the actual punching. In the center is an opening in which is placed an adjustable die. At the back is an upright edge,

comparable to the one at the back of the arranging board, except that this one is adjustable. The table is furnished with wooden boards on the right and left sides with revolving rollers at the ends to facilitate the moving of the book from left to right.

2. An arm above the punch table and attached to it at the back. The front portion of it is directly over the die in the table. It is in this front section of the arm that the chisel for punching out the perforations is located.

3. A wooden pedal connected with the arm and attached to the base section of the machine. It must be depressed with the foot for each perforation to be made. This action is relayed to the assembly at the end of the arm so that the chisel is forced down into the die. It is vital that this die be carefully positioned so that the keenly sharpened chisel is perfectly lined up with it.

The punching of the organ books proceeds as follows: the roll of paper on which the music is written . . . in technical terms called the "type" . . . is fastened to the folds of the book section by section. The cardboard with the type fastened to it is then placed on the table in such a way that the top edge is pressed against the adjustable upright at the back of the table. By pushing down on the foot pedal now one can cause the chisel in the mechanism at the end of the overhead arm to pierce the paper and cardboard and penetrate into the die, thus cutting sharply-defined rectangular holes. The chisels all have the same width; 4 mm, a size calculated to admit the key of the clavier but not its neighbors, but they come in varying lengths, to wit 5, $5\frac{1}{2}$, 6, 7, 8, 9, 10, and 12 mm. By changing chisels carefully, one can punch out holes of the desired length. Each time the cutter is changed, the die naturally has to be altered correspondingly, for if this were not done, one would punch ragged holes in the type and the book.

Gijs Perlee Sr. busy punching out an organ book with the "type" machine. (photograph by Paul Huf, Jr., commissioned by Grolsche Bierbrouwerij N. V. at Enschede) Editor's note: Bierbrouwerij means beer brewery.

199

For holes that have to be longer than 12 mm, one uses the 12 mm cutter and punches it through the book the required number of times in succession, moving the book forward each time approximately one cm. It is, of course, of the utmost importance that the holes be carefully punched in perfect alignment with the keys which will have to spring up into them, for when the instrument plays the keys must track in the center of the perforations. To attain this, the guide at the back of the punching table must be adjusted by means of a handle; i.e., moved towards or away from the operator very small distances, which must correspond precisely with the distance between the keys of the clavier. To position this guide accurately, a notched raised ridge is fixed permanently to the table; these notches spaced the same distance apart as are the keys of the clavier, or 17 to approximately 6 cm. Now by moving the adjustable guide according to the notches in the raised ridge and keeping the book firmly pressed against it at all times, one can punch holes in the book at the correct points. Thus if one has to punch a book for a 56-key organ, it will be necessary to move the guide over 56 notches of the raised rim back and forth, placing it carefully in a notch each time, in order to be able to punch holes over the entire width of the book.

We feel that we have now adequately explained the principles of the punching-out process and shall omit any additional details and the complications which may arise.

We should, however, like to mention one more related detail. It happens over and over that a passage of a book needs to be repeated. It is not necessary for the arranger to write it down twice on the type; instead, he can mark the passage to be repeated clearly (with colored pencil, for instance) and indicate its beginning with a clear vertical line. When one gets to this line during the punching out of the book, the "repeat type" is placed on the blank part of the book and is then used as a stencil, with colored liquid painted over the holes in it. Then it is removed and the painted patterns on the book are punched out.

When the whole tune is finally finished, one has besides the book a punched-out type. This is carefully preserved, for it can be used in preparing another book if the organ-renter concerned has more instruments with the same scale, by the same stencil process described above. In practice this occurs mostly with organs having the 56-key scale. When the type is made for a one-of-a-kind instrument, however, (such as the Arab, Zaza, and Mouthorgan) it is still advisable to keep it. Imagine, for instance, that the book was lost or worn out. A new one could easily be made from the original type.

When the new book has finally been finished, it still may not be played right away, for first it has to be shined up with the fragrant shellac, a treatment designed to make the cardboard very hard where the holes are punched. This is because the cardboard at the end of the perforations has to exert enough pressure on the keys which have popped up into them to force them back down again, and experience has shown that this is the point of the greatest wear and tear. To keep the cardboard at these points from being torn, the book is shellacked.

Care has to be taken also that the keys of the clavier run as smoothly as possible. They must always be ground round and smooth on top and at the back and must also move smoothly up and down in the clavier.

When finally the book has absorbed a layer of shellac and has dried . . . to which purpose it is put on its backside on the floor in fanlike fashion . . . the exciting moment of the first performance is there. Whenever one enters an organ workshop and smells shellac, one experiences a good feeling for two reasons: the smell of the shellac is delicious in itself, and furthermore, it means a premier is drawing near.

And how will it be? Will the book turn out to be a masterpiece? Too bad, readers, that we cannot let you share in this experience . . . but we can do something else. We can share with you, by way of illustration, the partial reproduction of an existing type; the scale of the organ for which it was made; and the same music in standard music notation. We hope in this way to enable you to read the music off the type. To give you a little assistance there is the scale, which you can move along over the type (remember that the top edge of the scale should coincide perfectly with the top edge of the type), and the music notation written out directly under the corresponding measure of the type.

The following material will help give you a better understanding of the illustrative material found in the back of this book. The type is to be read from left to right like a regular book and like regular music notation. Our initiated organ friends will now be very much surprised, for they are accustomed to reading them exactly the opposite, from right to left. When a book is to be played it is lying to the left of the clavier, and the top leaf is picked up, drawn toward the right, and clamped into the mechanism. Thus the first chord punched in the book lies at the extreme right, the following one is to the left, etc. Our organ friends must excuse us, however, for turning the type around exactly 180 degrees for the benefit of the uninitiated so that it could be read from left to right. In this way the type can be read in the easiest manner, measure for measure, together with the music written underneath. It is made to the scale of 1:2,5, so it is $\frac{2}{5}$ the length and width of life-size. Actually, the original is 32 cm wide and each $\frac{3}{4}$ measure runs 5 cm. The sharp rectangular holes here are 1.6 wide, while in the original, they are 4 mm.

The scale, which is also made to 1:2,5 and so in reality is also 32 cm long, is that of the 89-key Gavioli organ. You can see on this scale from bottom to top distinctly indicated the keys for the violin-piano register and the cancel, the ground basses, the conductor, the accompaniment, the violins, the piccolos, the bass drum, the trombones, the highest piccolo f″, the first snaredrum stick, the baritone horns, the second snaredrum stick, and the register forte. You can see, we have chosen an elaborate, but therefore interesting scale. Where the registers are concerned, we have made it easy for you, for we have to do only with the register violin-piano, whereby the violins and accompaniment play normally, and the forte register, whereby the violins are augmented with mixtures and the accompaniment with reed works. The other sections play on normal all the time, so the use of the registers has no influence on them. The remarkable thing about the 89-key Gavioli scale is that besides the violin in the melody and the baritone horn in the harmony, the piccolos play a separate part, a kind of "super-melody". It is noteworthy that in the Gavioli organ for which this type was arranged, the "Grote Gavioli" (see page 247), the violins and piccolos overlap beautifully, because violin pipes have been added to the 5 lowest piccolos (c, c♯, d, d♯, e), pipes which connect with the high b of the violins. Or, to phrase it differently, in the five notes mentioned the violins and the piccolos overlap. It is, of course, very easy to make a glissando from the lowest violin (g) to the highest piccolo (f″). The sound character changes so gradually and smoothly that the transition from violin to piccolo is in no way jarring. Another specialty of the 89-key Gavioli organs is that for each of the eight trombones, separate keys have been reserved. In most organs the trombones work on a special register. When it is drawn, they play on the keys of the basses. The great advantage of the 89-key Gavioli scale is that the trombones, especially since they work on separate keys, can be used differently from the ground basses. Thus, if the latter last a whole beat, they can be accentuated by trombones which last only half a beat, giving the effect in the bass group referred to in music notation as fp (forte-piano) or sf (sforzando). These bass notes acquire a strong character through this device. Moreover, it is possible to fortify some basses with trombones and others not, depending on which ones need accenting. You can see on the type that the basses in the measures 3, 5, 7, 9, 11, and 13 are thus strengthened, while those in 4, 6, 8, 10, 12, and 14 are not.

In ordinary notation, the basses and accompaniment are on the lower staff, the violins and piccolos on the middle one, and the baritones on the top. Below the lowest staff the signs for the trombones (V), bass drum (O), and snare drum (⸫⸫⸫⸫⸫⸫) are given. In order to make the whole illustration as clear as possible, we have usually omitted the lowest g of the violins, where this was used only to strengthen the accompaniment, and also we did not copy the harmony on the lowest staff where this was amplified by the accompaniment, as in measures 23 through 30.

The music used in the illustration is the "Dans van de harlekijn" (Waltz of the Jumping Jack) by the Amsterdam organist-carillonneur Bernard Drukker, awarded the first prize at the street organ-composition contest held in Utrecht in 1959. Only the first 30 measures are given here on the type. After an introduction of two measures, the main melody starts with violins and piccolos imitating the stiff, rhythmic leaps of the Jumping Jack in staccato . . . however else could they be! In measure 15, he suddenly makes a mighty leap, at which moment a counter-melody starts on the baritone. Now its slow, heavy melody has exactly the opposite effect from the high, intense jumps of the piccolos and violins in the main melody. While these jumps descend, the harmony moves in the opposite direction, creating a simple threefold contrast between melody and harmony: high and intense against low and dark; short and powerful against slow and wide; descending movement against ascending movement. This is how the specific capacities of the street organ can be displayed in traditional counterpoint. In measures 19 through 22 the motif of measures 15 through 18 is repeated, but now everything is brought in; i.e., the forte register is put to work, also the bass drum with cymbal (first beat of each measure) and snare drum (continuous roll over all four measures). In measures 23 through 30, the main melody is repeated, but this time in a different version, the violins playing in legato and the piccolos in groups of repeated short notes. Thus the effect described on page 197 is achieved. The most important point here is that the baritone now calls for your attention. By this variation of the main melody and the new harmony playing against it, the music remains fascinating to the listener.

It is needless to note that in these 30 measures shown on the "type" we could not possibly exhaust the many possibilities for combinations and variations in arranging for an 89-key Gavioli. There are many more. For example: violin and baritone can be combined in a melody which sounds heavy and sonorous, but also softly radiant, while at the same time it can be surrounded by fast runs and trills on the piccolo. One could also have the baritone and piccolos together in the main melody, this unison then being at once dark and heavy as well as silvery and shining, while the violins play the harmony. And let us not forget the possibility of having a march motif played by basses, trombones, baritones, accompaniment with reeds and possibly the lowest violins, while a lively obligatto is furnished by short and quickly-repeated chords on the violins and fast glissandos on the piccolos. However, it is not within the compass of this work to go into the subject any more deeply at this time. On the contrary, it seems to us that after this extensive introduction nothing stands in the way of a fruitful study of the illustrative material.

The Preservation of 11
the Pierement

Is there a danger that the pierement will disappear? At the beginning of part II we announced that this question would be the starting point of the last chapter. The answer, unfortunately, is that there is some danger, for the period from 1945-1960 which we are now about to discuss stands out especially because of the battle for the preservation of the pierement, a battle which is still being fought by all possible means. One of these is the publication of this book. Actually, it is just for this reason that it is better to have an exclamation instead of a question as the springboard of this chapter. The pierement must not disappear! Anyone who is not yet convinced of this after reading the previous chapters should give some thought to the following:

The Meaning of the Pierement in Our Society

The pierement has many facets of importance to our society. We shall point out six of these.

1. The pierement affords many people musical enjoyment. Do not underestimate the number of those who seek and find satisfaction for their musical needs in the pierement! We are thinking in this regard particularly of those people who are blessed with a natural musicality, but who, due to social and economic circumstances, were not able to develop their inborn talent by taking music lessons, playing an instrument, or going regularly to concerts by good orchestras. Experience during the past 15 years has shown us that the percentage of people who feel primarily attracted to street organs is at least as large as that of regular concertgoers. For this group in particular the disappearance

of the street organ would be a calamity comparable to that of the Concertgebouworkest for the regular concert-goers! However, while in this vein our thoughts go to musically inclined youngsters also. Isn't the thought of spending a few moments with this group of music lovers rather pleasant? Many of those people who think they have long since outgrown the period in which they loved the pierement have to admit that they discovered the true beauty of music for the first time in the pierement, and that it played an important role in the period of their youth when their musical comprehension was gradually being awakened.

2. The pierement also has an important function in an aesthetic and folkloristic sense. An undeniable charm is radiated not only from the music but also from the outward appearance of the organ. There is a nearly universal appreciation of the beautiful old building facades, the bridges, and canals which are fortunately still (!) numerous in Amsterdam. How much more moving this beauty is, however, when it serves as the background for a pierement painted in fresh colors and furnished with graceful carved figures, standing near a canal or being pushed across one of the bridges. The spectators at the 26 organ meets which have been organized since 1954 have carried away with them an indelible memory of the pierement facades and the spell they cast. At these times numerous organs come together and the spectators number into the thousands. Behind the facades of the organs, which are lined up "bumper to bumper", rise the stately old buildings of a market-place or the fresh-looking trees and bushes of a park, depending on where the festival is being held. If it happens to be a park, then the inherently beautiful color-schemes of the shrubs and flowers are themselves pushed into the background by the fantastic colors, now flamboyantly vivid,

now delicately pastel, of the scrolls, flourishes, pillars, roses, and streamers which lend themselves as settings for the sometimes quasi-innocent but again, also shamelessly wanton and provocative carved figures. And what splendor when at dusk the instruments are lighted by numerous floodlights!

3. The pierement is peculiarly suited to the creation of an atmosphere of festivity and conviviality perhaps best summed up as "Gemutlichkeit". The first to come to mind would be the national holidays, where the unique good cheer of the street organ is synonymous with gaily flapping flags, colorful decorations, brilliant illumination, merry carillon music, and parades marching by playing snappy tunes. Is not then the pierement an essential ingredient in the mixture of pomp and festivity which has such a galvanizing effect on our national pride and sense of freedom? Also at special occasions such as weddings and other family celebrations, masked balls, neighborhood festivities, ceremonial openings of roads, bridges, etc., the street organ can play an important role, and not only out-of-doors, but also inside it can be a welcome element in the general happiness. Even in the ordinary, everyday life of the city the street-organ can contribute immeasurably by the good atmosphere and the pleasant feeling it creates. The children who play tag in the streets and dart about the organ experience it, as well as the students who (paying in advance) generously give the organ grinder their collected pocket-money to have him come and play for a prolonged period during a boring lesson! Often the teachers offer him even more money if he will please disappear with his instrument as quickly as possible. Of course, a dedicated organ grinder could never honorably accept such a proposal! Housewives performing their sometimes so boring household chores find, too, how much the pierement can brighten things up and offer welcome relief. The periodic arrival of the street

organ man spells a break in the rut her daily work tends to become.

4. The pierement has a much deeper, more fundamental meaning for Dutch expatriates and their descendents all over the world, many of whom undoubtedly feel a need to strengthen their ties with the homeland and, together with their fellow Dutchmen, renew all those things which bind them together, even though they consider the other country their new motherland. How welcome the old, familiar pierement is when it appears in their midst! Well, as far as that is concerned, these Dutch people have had nothing to complain about during the last fifteen years. The list of organs which have been sent abroad for the benefit of these people when a typically Dutch flavor was needed to liven things up grows steadily. Many of them have disappeared to other countries for good, to return to the Netherlands at most temporarily to be restored. "De Mattenklopper" (The Carpetbeater) moved to Aruba; "Het Glaskistje" (The Glasscase) to Indonesia, "Het Schapenkopje" (The Sheephead) to Norway; "Het Waterduikertje" (The Water Diver) to South Africa; "De Paraplu" (The Umbrella) to Canada, and "De Oosterse Dame" (The Oriental Lady) to America. The "Vier Kolommen" (Four Columns) was sent to the Dutch in Michigan; "De Chimmy" went to enliven the Holland Fair in Philadelphia and "De Grote Buik" (The Big Belly) was presented to Paramaribo by the mayor of Amsterdam, D'Ailly. Although this interest abroad in our street organs makes us very happy, we are forced to make one admission: we shall definitely have to call a halt to the exodus of our street organs out of Holland, for we cannot afford to export street organs. We must pay atten-

---

A fair organ built by Carl Frei in Waldkirch after the second World War.

210

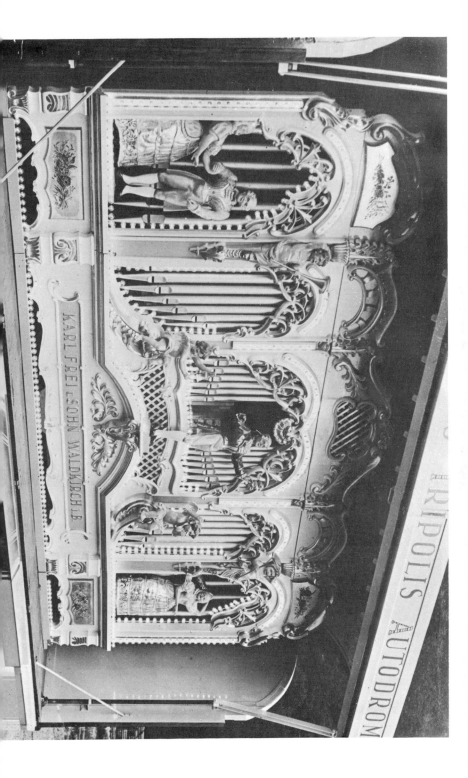

tion to our own interior situation first, which will become self-evident as we progress in this last chapter. We should like to encourage the system of tours . . . that is, *temporary* trips of street organs in order to satisfy the people abroad. Fortunately, this aspect of the situation has been improving in recent years. We shall come back to this subject later.

5. The pierement is often a source of inspiration for creative artists. In the first place we think of composers of original street-organ music, such as Carl Frei and the competitors in the street organ music contest held in Utrecht in the summer of 1959, as well as the composers and lyricists of the numerous popular songs in which our pierement has a role: "Als van d'Amsterdamse grachten het pierement verdwijnt" (If the Pierement Disappeared from the Grachten of Amsterdam); "Speelt het orgel op het pleintje" (The Organ is Playing on the Square); "Het lied van het pierement" (The Song of the Pierement); "Als 't orgel verschijnt" (When the Organ Appears); "Daar is de orgelman" (There is the Organ Man); the "orgelliedje" (Organ Song) of brother Laetantius, etc.

And then there are the film people! Several of these creative artists have already been inspired by the pierement. Do you remember the film "The True and the Brave" alias "Betrayed"? The subject of this movie was the liberation of Holland by the allied troops in 1944 and 1945. In order to give the background music a typically Dutch flavor, the pierement was given an important part. The organs "De Drie Pruiken" and "De Gouwe" performed about ten different versions of the song "Johnny Come Back", so that they had a role similar to the zither in "The Third Man". The inspiration of the pierement makes itself felt even more clearly when an organ has a part not only in the sound track, but also in the visual part as well. Here we think first,

212

of course, of the film "Pierement" by Teunissen, which was a triumph in 1933, the period when sound films were first being made. We cannot but feel proud that the pierement was one of the first means whereby a pioneer in motion pictures exploited sound. In that short film one heard and saw how a sleeply Jordaan (a famous section of Amsterdam) came to life more and more because of a travelling pierement. The inevitable dynamic effect of the organs on the life rhythm of the population is beautifully suggested in this film!

A pregnant role is given in pierement in "Ciske the Rat". At the beginning of this film, one first hears and then sees "De Mondorgel" playing. The climax comes in the scene where Ciske stabs his mother fatally with a bread knife. Immediately after one sees the flash of the knife, the eye of the camera is trained on the organ "De Drie Pruiken" with its three stiff carved figures, for it has just started playing in front of Ciske's house at this dramatic moment. With a penetrating glissando in the violin-celeste, the organ begins a haunting waltz melody, in which a short motif returns again and again symbolizing the thrust of the knife. How splendid is the contrast between the image of Ciske, who throws the knife at his mother with a brusque arm movement, and that of the conductor of "De Drie Pruiken", who indicates the beginning of this short motif each time with his baton. About the movie "Het wonderbaarlijke leven van Willem Parel" (The Wonderful Life of Willem Parel), which from a "pierementological" point of view was not very successful, we shall say nothing, in spite of the parade of twelve Amsterdam pierements from Rembrandt Square to the living quarters of the mayor on Herengracht. This does not in any way detract from our admiration of the character of Parel himself. Here also we must not omit the artist Wim Sonneveld, who was inspired to an artistic creation by a pierement and the man who played it. We are very grateful for this work, even if only for the enormous amount of publicity which he gave street organs in his "tweede Ik" (Second I).

To return briefly to films. Have you seen what part the street organ plays in "Operatie Amsterdam" (Operation Amsterdam) and "Dagen can mijn jaren" (Days of My Years)? Concerning the latter, however, we have to admit that our appreciation of the movie itself is overshadowed by our disappointment over the fact that the function of the street organ was not developed at all as it was originally conceived by Max de Haas. It was supposed to be symbolic of that which continues and is imperishable in life, in the midst of world-shaking events, fashions, and fads. When we saw the premier, however, we wondered whether the organ had not lost, rather than won, the battle! It did appear on the scene as it was planned, but the music was more and more drowned out by the background music, which had been produced by the most modern means and thus clashed with the romanticism of the pierement.

In conclusion, we have this to say about films and film-makers. When will a Dutch movie director work out the obvious idea of making a documentary entirely devoted to the pierement? For that matter, there are other categories of creative artists to whom the pierement so far has not been a source of inspiration. To mention one, we are still waiting for a good novel dealing with a street organ or the life of an organ grinder. Still, who knows what may yet come about when this chapter is read some day by a writer of novels?

6. The pierement can be very useful in advertising. The first thing to mention in this area would be the release of certain musical compositions, especially in the lighter vein, to the general public. The street organ is eminently suited

to this purpose, in which it can be likened to the radio. In their endeavors to push the theme-songs from new movies and turn them into hit tunes, the movie companies have had books made of them for organs. Some of these melodies have come from "Mariandel", "Look for the Silver Lining", "Sterren stralen overal" (Stars Are Shining Everywhere), and "Hi Lili Hi lo". The "Roverssymphonie" (Robbers' Symphony) was another which was given this treatment. Although this music was originally known only by the comparatively few who saw the film of the same name, it became familiar to a great many more people when arrangements of it were played on various organs.

The pierement can be effective in other types of advertising, too. It can serve to attract people when some charitable or cultural drive is on, as when the Edam carillon was in need of restoration, for example. A lottery was organized, and many chances were sold at the Dam in Amsterdam, where the concert organ "De Grote Gavioli" functioned as piece de milieu. Many more chances would have been sold if the grand prize had been made a street organ, but perhaps this idea can be used at a future date. The fact that money can be collected quite successfully for charitable purposes with the help of the street organ was demonstrated quite conclusively, to single out one instance, in the big anti-rheumatism drive held in Amsterdam on Sept. 22, 1956, in which the climax was a large gathering of all the Amsterdam organs at the Dam.

We hope to have shed some light on the various aspects of the significance of the pierement to us and our society. However, we think we may anticipate a reaction on the part of some of our readers to the effect that it must be so universally recognized and appreciated an element in our Dutch folklore, and must have such a secure niche in the history of our social structure, that its preservation would be a matter of course. How dangerous such an attitude is to our cause! The only thing which is self-evident, and in reality is generally conceded, is that the pierement must be preserved. We all agree on that. That this will actually come to pass is far from being as certain. No, for the preservation of the street organ, we need not only the joint energy of all real organ friends (including those who thus far have let a misplaced feeling of timidity keep them from expressing themselves!), but even more specifically, the understanding cooperation and assistance of the Dutch government and people. That we cannot do without it in the battle to save the pierement should be self-evident from the following survey of the development of

THE PIEREMENT IN THE PERIOD FROM 1945 TO 1960.

When we look back on the events of the past fifteen years in the organ world, it is striking how each time a series of events brought disappointment and gloom, there always seemed to be something equally joyful and encouraging as a counterbalance.

The come-back of the pierement in 1945 was most dramatic at the very outset. In May of 1945 when the populace of Amsterdam thought the city was completely liberated, they went to the Dam in great numbers and took "Het Snotneusje" (I am sure our readers remember the meaning of this one!) along to help express their exhuberance. They could not know, however, that in the building of the "Grote Club" (Large Club) there still remained a group of Germans. After a time they opened fire on the crowd and the people scattered in all directions, trying to find a hiding place anywhere they could. A num-. ber of them managed to hide behind "Het Snotneusje", to which they probably owe their lives, for it was discovered

An eloquent scene from the film "The Wonderful Life of Willem Parel". The sign says "These organs are our greatest treasure, where're they go, they give one pleasure."

217

later that the little organ was riddled with bullets. One of them is still preserved at the museum, "From Music Box to Pierement". "Het Snotneusje" is thus not only the smallest, but also the most valiant of all the Amsterdam pierement!

After the liberation the organs reappeared on the streets everywhere to heighten the gaiety of the celebrations, most of them fortunately having survived the war. But, how were things with the manufacturers? It appeared that in 1945 only two of the large Belgian organ factories were still in existence, Burssens and De Cap. However, no more instruments have been made in these two factories which could be exported as street organs, for in Belgium the pre-war dance organs were considered more and more old-fashioned. Instead of these, mechanical musical instruments of quite a different calibre have been introduced into the dancehalls and cafes. These can best be characterized as mechanical jazz orchestras. Like the pre-war dance organs, they performed primarily music with a strong rhythm and were rather large. The facades had complete drum installations in the center, with saxophones and accordions to the left and right. Organs were built in this same style later on, which produced music electronically. These modern instruments, however, are really beyond the purview of this chapter. We only mention them at all to explain that the developments in Belgium after 1945 have been such that no more instruments at all have been built in the style of our traditional street organs. Nor did Carl Frei manufacture more of them after the war. In 1945 he had to leave our country, and he returned to his native land to start a completely new organ concern in Waldkirch im Bresgau with his son. Since then father and son Frei have produced beautiful instruments in collaboration with the wood-carver, Wilhelm List. These organs, with facades of

218

v?rying styles, have all been designed for German fair concessions, however, and all have had the large size and the majestic sound characteristic of this type of instrument. No more street organs have been made in the new factory of Carl Frei & Sohn.

The upshot of it is that since 1945, no more factories have existed which were equipped to turn out a line of street organs as the French and Belgian firms and the Breda factory of Carl Frei had done during the first 40 years of this century. Concerning the stock of pierement still in existence in Holland, the warning: "O Nederland let op uw saeck!" (O Holland, Watch Your Interests! . . . the title of an old Dutch patriotic song) is all too appropriate. However, after sounding this alarm, there are still two questions which in all fairness must be asked. First, could not Burssens, De Cap, and Carl Frei & Sohn have built street organs for the Netherlands as they did before the war if they had received orders for them, even though their stock production was of a different genre altogether? An affirmative answer can be given in principle. Under the circumstances, however, it is understandable that they received no orders. In the first place, a new instrument would be exorbitantly expensive as a result of the high cost of materials and labor, because of having fewer people with the requisite abilities, and because of the much less favorable rate of exchange since the war. In the second place, Holland had no desire to increase the existing number of organs already in the country. But could they manage to maintain these old instruments? This is the second of the two questions inspired by the above warning, for, in order to keep them playing, craftsmen were needed who were capable of handling the inevitable restorations and repairs. Indeed! Happily, it soon became evident that at least we did not have cause to worry on that score. To compensate somewhat for the sombre fact that the large pre-war street organ builders were now gone, there now appeared a particularly joyful phenomenon: it seemed that Holland possessed craftsmen who were not only capable of restoring organs adequately, but also had quite astonishing results with completely rebuilding them and even with the production of new registers of pipes, of which the new bourdons (you must have guessed!) especially are outstanding. What a remarkable ending to the history of the pierement from 1875 to today. While the origin and the rapid evolution of the street organ up to the second World War was entirely due to the continuous fruitful cooperation between Dutch rental agencies and foreign organbuilders, since the war the whole business, even including the actual building of organs, has been within the Netherlands itself. Surveying the whole picture from the earliest period up to the present, we see a gradual move from Italy (the home of Gavioli and Gasparini) to France (beginning period of the book organs) and Belgium (zenith of the industry) and finally, to the Netherlands. Thus the originally international street organ business (we intentionally exclude fair and dance organs here) has been concentrated in our country since 1945. Of course, the Dutch organ builders did not just appear out of thin air as if by magic. On the contrary, the most important ones had already received their training and experience largely before the war, usually through working in some organ concern in their youth where they had learned all the tricks of the trade. Some of them had already proven themselves before the war by building and voicing new registers to replace old-fashioned ones or those whose tone quality was no longer suitable. Before 1940 the achievements of these Dutch craftsmen, however, were more or less overshadowed by the steady and ostentatious arrival of the new Belgian and Carl Frei organs.

The history of the Dutch street organ builders largely runs parallel to that of the rental agencies, for practical experience has shown that the only rental concerns that managed to survive were those that were able to take care of their own instruments, overhaul them, and if necessary do complete rebuilding. One individual in Rotterdam who started a rental agency after the war, although himself not an expert and employing no one who was, found he was not able to do much more than sell all the organs which had become his property during the war. Fortunately, the most outstanding of them, such as "De Gouwe", "De Grote Witte", "De Paraplu" (The Umbrella), "De Kerstkrans" (The Christmas Wreath), and "De Blauwe Pilaar", fell into good hands and thus were preserved.

Of all the pre-war rental agents whom we have met in the previous chapters, only two were successful in continuing business after the war. These were the two grandsons of the original founder, Leon Warnies, by name Henk Mohlmann, the son of Susanna Warnies (now 86 years old), and Gijs Perlee, the son of Leontine Ermina Warnies and Gijs Perlee, Sr., who had both died.

The stock of the Mohlmann firm on Brouwersgracht, which had comprised mainly of Carl Frei organs even before the war, was now augmented with still more Frei instruments which were acquired from the previous rental agents Louis Holvoet and Willem van Jaaren. Among them were "De Negentiger", "De Vier Kolommen", "De Cementmolen", "De Bloemenmeid", "De Sik", "De Duif", and "De Gavioli" . . . mouthwatering acquisitions!

At the headquarters of Perlee on Westerstraat things began to go differently. This concern, which could hardly hold its own before the war in the face of such mighty competitors as Willem van Jaaren, now began to branch out steadily. Year by year the number of instruments in the stock of the company grew. Regularly old organs already owned by Perlee, or newly-purchased ones were completely rebuilt, after which they reappeared spanking new on the streets. The steady growth of this firm to by far the largest one in the Netherlands is due not only to the negative factor that the biggest competitors of before 1940 fell away, but also, and much more significantly, to the positive force of the fine craftsmanship, the keen business acumen, and the consistent drive with which business activities were conducted. Until 1950 the very capable organ builder, Karel Struys, also a grandson of Leon Warnies, Sr., was a member of the team back of this flourishing enterprise. He was born of the first marriage of Leontine Ermina Warnies and so is a half-brother of Gijs Perlee. We particularly wish to acknowledge the beautiful bourdon registers which he built. We shall mention only one example of them, but it is a telling one: "De Arabier" (The Arab). After Struys started his own business as organ builder in 1950, Perlee's sons Gijs and Cor gradually became the key men in the business, earned through insight and craftsmanship. Gijs specialized entirely in the painting and restoration of the facades and cases, while the younger Cor penetrated into the musical and construction secrets of organ building, and learned to construct and voice pipes while still very young. The bourdon registers of "De Drie Pruiken" and the "Labre Organ" of Eindhoven (a city in the south of Holland) are his work. Some of the organs bought and restored since the war by Perlee are "De Vier Jaargetijden" (The Four Seasons) and "De IJzeren Hein" (Iron Henry), both 67-key Burssens; "De Zaza", "De Grote Witte" and "De Paraplu", all by Koeningsberger; "De Pod", "De Gouwe", and "De Hindenburg", 90-key instruments by Carl Frei; "De Kerstkrans" by De Cap, "De Puntkap" (The Pointed Cap), a 72-key Frei, and "De Mondorgel", "De Cello", and "Het Snuffeltje" (Snoopy).

The scope of this book is not such as to allow us to list the many restorations done by Perlee on organs which he

222

owned prior to 1940. However, we shall later on in this chapter tell the story of the most famous one in his collection, "De Arabier".

Besides the two Amsterdam rental agencies, a third one has been founded in the past ten years in Hilversum by father and son Gosslings. The manner in which they have built up this business and enlarged it deserves respect. After starting out with a few organs of their own which they worked on the streets, they began to specialize in repair and rebuilding, while at the same time adding to their own stock of instruments. Now among those in their collection are to be found "De Blauwe Pilaar" (90-key Frei), "De Radiostad" (Radio City, a rebuilt Dewyn dance organ which originally could be heard in the cafe of the former rental agent Winter in Zaandam, a town near Adam, for years after the war), "De Kameel" (The Camel, a rebuilt De Cap), "De Accordeola", with accordions in both left and right side cases, "De Limonaire", and "De Grote Beer" (The Big Bear).

Now let us devote our attention to street organ builders Jan Gillet and Jac Minning of Rotterdam. The former has earned recognition since the war with his very up-to-date, snappy-sounding organs containing three accordions and specifically for two of his creations, "De Oranjestad" (The Orange City, a reference to the royal family), and "De Kleine Beer" (The Little Bear). The instruments rebuilt by Minning with great craftsmanship are immediately recognizable by their names. They shine like planets in the heavens of the organ world, as is indicated by their names . . . "De Jupiter", the 67-key Gavioli which has become one of the most beloved of all the street organs, "De Mercurius", and "De Saturnus". In the case of one of his restorations, the rechristening did not stick. Of course not, for who could stand for "Uranus" as a substitute name for such a famous and old organ as "De Turk"?

The men discussed so far have concerned themselves with the pierement proper, even though Henk Mohlmann is a welcome guest in the fair world. Many fair managers have him service their organs. Louis van Deventer of Brummen, about whom we shall have more to say later in this chapter, has specialized exclusively in the restoration and rebuilding of fair organs, while W. Stelleman-Berge of Eindhoven is well-known for his work with dance instruments. He will also be mentioned again. Rein van den Broek from Gorcum, a small town near Rotterdam, is a man who threw himself energetically into the trading in and rebuilding of dance organs. The street organs which he himself worked in Gorcum, one of which was "De Arkel", were also dance instruments which he had rebuilt. Rein van den Broek is one of those disinterested people who work regularly for the "Kring van Draaiorgelvrienden" (Circle of Friends of the Street Organ) in such projects as the bringing of the "Aalster Gavioli" from Aalst (a small town in Belgium) to the museum in Utrecht. (We regret that we are unable to elaborate on this most adventuresome mission, in which we got stuck first at the border, and later on near the Merwede (a river in the southern part of Holland) in a pouring rain with our precious cargo.)

Are you quite dizzy with all these names of organs and organ builders, dear readers? If so, we are sorry, but our intention was only to show you by this elaboration what great strides have been taken by the Dutch in this field since the second World War. The fact that the number of rental agencies has decreased so much because of the war does not necessarily need to give rise to pessimism, for the ones still in business have more than enough organs to meet the demand. And if there should arise a much greater call

---

The Gavioli street organ, "De Jupiter", which has become famous in Haarlem.

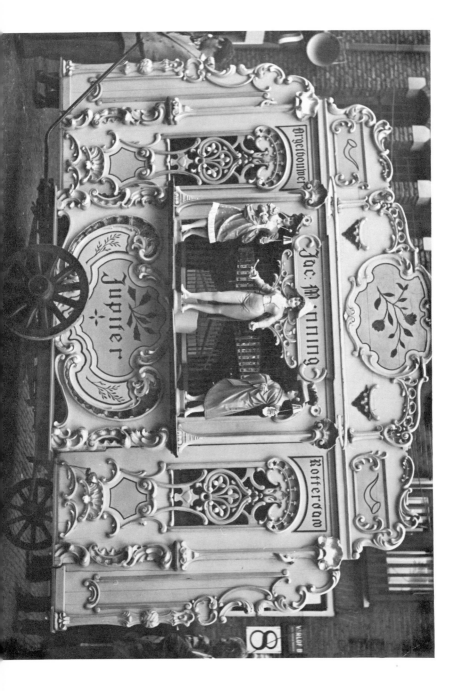

for them eventually, there are more in storage which could be rebuilt and put back in service. But if it will ever get that far . . . ? This is a question about which we do worry, and it is bound up with the way business is conducted with license holders and their crews.

After the war life was not very easy for the organ grinders and collectors. The difficulties which they encountered were a direct result of the upheaval in economics and the social structure. The companies were forced to increase their rental fees drastically after the war, sometimes even doubling them from fl. 15.00 to fl. 30.00 per week. It could not be helped. The cost of labor and materials had risen so terrifically that the few agencies that were left could not have gone on without compensating for higher costs by charging higher rent. The value of money was just not the same any longer as it had been before the war. Of course not, you will say. That is self-evident. But why, if the situation is so obvious, did people not act accordingly when giving money to an organ man? For many continued to give no more than the traditional prewar "penny". Was this because the organ grinders were the only ones who had not officially increased their fee? This they could not do, and anyway, their motto is to be the well-known "Dank u bolleefd!" (Thank you kindly!) under all circumstances.

Another significant factor was . . . and is . . . the improvement of the picture in employment. Before the war, many men decided to play a street organ for a living simply because there was no other work to be had. The postwar situation was much changed.

Another closely-related factor is the significant improvement in social conditions, which has caused the job of organ grinder to become less attractive than those in which one assumes the position of employee. The organ man is independent and the social benefits are not the same for him. In view of the fact that there are more jobs available, the postwar organ grinder is often pleasantly accosted with "Why don't you go to work for a change?", which needs no further elaboration. If they all did *work* in a different field (and we say *work* most emphatically, for making a living with an organ is of course work, and very hard work at that!), then there would be no more organs on the streets! Could that possibly be the wish of those people who voice such hateful thoughts? Or does this hypochondriac wish to reveal the drive of the would-be social reformer?

For organ men in the big cities comes the added obstacle of the ever-increasing flow of traffic and the consequent lack of parking space for the instruments. The result is often that on the busiest streets, where having a permanent stand is most lucrative, there is no place to stop without being in the way of traffic, while in the quieter ones where one is still allowed to park an organ, the spaces are usually taken up by cars. Because of these traffic problems, police regulations have become more strict, and also more and more main streets in our large cities are forbidden to organs altogether. As the police have to give increasingly more attention to the solution of all kinds of urgent traffic problems, less thought can be given to the interests of the organ people. And don't forget for a moment that the "attention" which the police devote to organs is purely negative! It is not their duty to see to it that the organ grinder gets any kind of preferential treatment. No, their only goal is to keep them from being a nuisance. A further facet of this relationship to the law is that it sometimes happens that the police react too severely and with blanket prohibitions when certain individual organ grinders transgress, and thereby hurt the licensees who behave themselves and do not create any difficulties at all.

Another unfavorable aspect of modern life, in cities especially, is that the pace is much faster and the people more keyed up and in a hurry than formerly, so that they just are not as receptive and interested in the organs as they once were, because of the loss of a certain inner quiet.

However, let us not dwell on the obstacles which have presented themselves in our large cities since 1945, but rather point out another of those remarkable and gratifying coincidences which are so characteristic of the period 1945-1960. For, to compensate for the rather unfavorable and sombre state of affairs in our largest cities, quite a favorable and encouraging development became apparent in a number of our medium-sized cities, a development which can be traced back to two causes.

Since 1952 there has been evident in our country a marked revival of interest in the pierement. We noticed the first signs of it when on Nov. 21, 1951, we gave a lecture on the history of the pierement in the Amsterdam municipal building to approximately 200 members of the club, "Our Amsterdam". In the hall the organ "De Negentiger" was on display, and among those present were Mr. Perlee and Mr. Mohlmann. Their presence would prove to be of great importance to the development of the style of organ fronts. As a curiosity we had taken along to the lecture two old, carved organ figures in particularly beautiful condition. As we stated in chapter 10, these carvings had become old-fashioned during the period between 1920-1930. These two had later on been used temporarily for another purpose when they were moved to the display window of a dress salon, where they were quite a success as mannequins. It was due to this fact that they were still impeccably dressed, or rather painted, when they were eventually returned to Mohlmann's shop. During the lecture we had left them standing in an unobtrusive spot covered with a cloth. When

The first organ to appear on the streets after the war decorated with carved figures: "The Three Wigs", now at Utrecht.

229

at the appropriate moment we unveiled the two figures (women) a long "aaah" rose spontaneously from the audience. In our memory we can still hear this heart-warming cry of delight and admiration, from which Mohlmann and Perlee each also drew his own conclusions. They reasoned, "If merely showing these carvings here arouses such enthusiasm, how will the public react when a pierement hits the streets decorated this way?" They lost no time. Mohlmann restored his organ "De Klok" (The Bell) and mounted the three carvings which are still to be seen in front of the new bourdon register which he built inside. Perlee at the same time built a practically new organ, "De Drie Pruiken" (The Three Wigs) which was christened thus because of the beautiful white wigs worn by the three male figures adorning the facade. In May, 1952 both "De Klok" and "De Drie Pruiken" were finished, and the hopes of the two entrepreneurs were far from dashed. The return of the figures to the organ fronts was generally so well received that since then, many license-holders have requested organs so equipped and have been willing to pay higher rent to get them! Soon old carvings that had been lying around for years were dug out of workshops and sheds, restored, and mounted on an organ.

Now that the figures have seduced us to a digression on the subject of style development, we do not wish to omit pointing out the following: while the periods 1900-1920 and 1920-1940 were characterized by certain strongly individual styles and fashions, this was no longer the case from 1945-1960. During the past few years the attitude that each organ should be restored as much as possible in its own original style has gained ground. A good example is the restoration of "De Turk", in which the original registers have been maintained and which has had its original carvings replaced as before. Even so, however, this principle has not been consistently adhered to. In the first place, sometimes bourdon registers in melody have been installed in organs that originally did not have them as in the "70 Burssens" and "De Mondorgel". This can be ascribed to the lasting popularity of this beautiful stop and to the practice common even before the war of giving an instrument a bourdon in melody wherever possible. In the second place, carvings have often been mounted on organs which never had had any, as in the case of "De Arabier", "De Gouwe", "De Cementmolen", "De Mondorgel", and other instruments built during the period 1920-1940. Although from the point of view of style we should disapprove of this practice, still we must admit that the figures look well even on these organs and do much to enhance their appearance.

But let us return to our lecture in the Amsterdam municipal building and tell you why it is of special significance to take note of it here. After those in attendance had absorbed certain aspects of our story, they reacted with the suggestion, "Let's organize a club of friends of the pierement!" Sheets were circulated for the signatures of those who were interested in the idea, and press, radio, record companies (in Dutch the word is "grammafoonplatenmaatschappijen"), and television began to turn their attention to the instrument and in no small way stimulated the newly-awakening interest. In many towns groups of enthusiasts got together, and in 1954 they organized themselves into the national "Kring van Draaiorgelvrienden" (Circle of Friends of the Street Organ). Some of these devotees went so far as to buy organs themselves and have them restored, which in many cases meant the preservation of the instruments involved. Here follows a list of pierements which have thus become private property: "De Jupiter", the property of Mr. Bank and Mr. Van Heyenoort in

Delft; "De Oranjestad" and "De Waterpoorter", now also the property of Mr. Van Heyenoort; "De Turk", bought by Van Heyenoort and now the property of Mr. Van der Bel in The Hague; "De Schietgaten", "De Stolwijker" (a name in the royal family), "De Engelenbak" (The Gallery), "De Twee Rozen", and even "De Negentiger", all bought by Mr. Paap of Arnhem; "De Sater" (The Devil), bought by ten organ friends in Middelburg; and "De Omke Romke", bought by a few organ friends in Bolsward.

Still, how is it to be explained that this new wave of enthusiasm for the organs was so pronounced in a number of our middle-sized cities, and that the pierement rose in esteem there above all? The explanation of this is connected with the outlined difficulties in which the license holders in the large cities and specifically the birthplace, Amsterdam, found themselves, and also with the healthy chauvinism of the citizens of those smaller cities. In order to clarify this for you, we can do no better than to relate the eventful story of the organ "De Arabier" which has become so famous in Groningen (northern part of Holland). This instrument was built by Pierre Verbeeck around 1926, and the scale he provided for it included 8 keys for basses, 10 for accompaniment, 22 (the usual number) for melody, 17 for counter-melody, and the remainder of the total of 75 for percussion, the registers, and extras. In the melody one could hear violin, flute-harmonique, carillon, and metallophone, and in the counter-melody were celeste, cello, baritone, bourdon, and flute 8. At the time there were no trombones in the instrument, and it had an accordion. On the side panels blazed forth an Arab to the left and to the right, one of his (many, we suppose) wives. In 1935 the organ

The Organ "De Arabier" grown famous in Groningen and not furnished with carved figures until 1954.

was bought by Perlee, Sr. from the previous owner, W. Prins of Alkmaar, and was rebuilt in a way which typifies the standards for street organs around 1935, as far as registers for melody were concerned. The flute-harmonique and the carillon were replaced by a bourdon and an especially beautiful one, built by Karel Struys. The accordion was removed and the violin register strengthened. In 1948 the instrument was again thoroughly rebuilt, this time acquiring the disposition it now has. Aside from internal improvements, it was altered as follows: to the basses was added a register of trombones, to the melody, a new register of violins, and to the counter-melody, a beautiful rank of celeste pipes. The flute 8 was replaced by a new register with a sound quality reminiscent of a biphone (mysterious and constantly working on tremolo) but in this case better labelled a "triphone" because three pipes speak for each note, an 8 foot, a 4 foot, and a duodecime (upper quint).

Thus the final disposition has turned out to include 8 basses and trombones, 10 accompaniments, 22 melody with violin, bourdon, and metallophone; 17 counter-melody with celeste, cello, baritone, and triphone, and rhythmic accent for the ensemble furnished by bass drum with cymbal, snare drum and castanets. As a result of this restoration "De Arabier" is a veritable jewel, and the fame which it enjoys now is richly deserved. The tonal effect is particularly pure, and the balance between the various registers is truly sublime. The melody is clear and transparent, but not too intense; the harmony, dark and sonorous, but not too heavy; and the basses and accompaniments furnish a distinct but not overwhelming foundation and harmonic background for the other sections. Furthermore, the entire instrument functions faultlessly in every respect, which was also the verdit of the expert, critical, and impartial judges in the six contests in which "De Arabier" has competed since August 11, 1954. It was awarded the highest score every time.

But now comes the remarkable part of the story. In spite of all his distinction, "De Arabier" was not particularly outstanding between 1948-1953 when it worked Amsterdam. The public just did not seem to pay any special attention to this organ. As we have mentioned before, it no longer took time out to listen quietly and critically to organs and weigh the qualities of one against the other. The rental companies drew the logical conclusion that a super collecting technique brings in more money than a super-pierement . . . except where the carved figures were concerned, for these caught even the casual glance of passers-by, especially children. There were none of these on "De Arabier", however, at least not at that time! So it happened that the Amsterdam licensees did not object when "De Arabier" was rented by Hendrik Elderman, a licensee from Groningen, in the summer of 1953. For the organ friends in Groningen (for there they had also formed a club) this was a red-letter day. Their enthusiasm over the arrival of the instrument knew no bounds, and they soon spread the word around that Holland's best organ was now in their city. One has to be a "Groninger" oneself to grasp the full significance of what it means to a native of Groningen to be first in one way or another, or as the well-known folk-song puts it, to be "number one". They were inordinately proud of their pierement, and they even organized special Arab-evenings in "De Harmonie" hall, where well-known public figures could grind out tunes to their hearts' content. The very beneficial result of this kind of thing was the disappearance of embarassment and self-consciousness. So "De Arabier" came to be the "jewel in a golden frame" with many admirers. This success enabled Elderman to beautify the organ even more, and also to add to the repertoire. Three figures were placed in front, to which two more were added later. For no other organ were so many new books bought by the licensee himself as there were for "De Arabier", and not only the usual hit tunes and special street organ compositions, but also many popular classical works especially suited to this instrument. Now in its extensive repertoire are such works as the overtures "Light Cavalry", "Gaza Ladra", "The Barber of Seville", "Poet and Peasant", "The Merry Wives of Windsor", and "Orpheus in the Underworld". The Groningers saw to it that the attention of the press, the radio, and the record companies be drawn to their favorite, so that it has become the most famous of the Dutch organs and has made tours to London, Denmark, Hamburg, Stuttgart, and . . . even to the island of Schiermonnikoog in honor of an 80-year old man whose heart's desire it was to hear a concert on "De Arabier" in his home on his birthday. In this way everyone has gotten to know this organ, with the exception of the little old lady who popped outside with an armful of scissors and knives when the organ came by and said, quite surprised, to Elderman, "I thought you were a scissors-grinder!" She had only caught a glimpse of the large wheel and jumped to conclusions.

After this very extensive example in Groningen, we shall have to be brief with similar cases. Rest assured, however, that "De Arabier" case does not stand alone, for the same thing happened to "De Jupiter" in Haarlem, "De Drie Pruiken" in Utrecht, "De Gouwe" in Leeuwarden, and "Da Zaza" in Amersfoort, and each has its own story. The most dramatic concerns "De Gouwe", which was so extensively damaged in 1957 in a collision that it had to be completely rebuilt. The sympathy of the population of Leeuwarden, indeed of all of Friesland, was enormous, and their joy was just as great when "De Gouwe" returned to Friesland's capital completely restored.

Street organ contest on May 5, 1955, in Haarlem. On the stage is the instrument with three accordions of Jan Gillet. In the background (completely visible) from left to right: "Het Witje" (The White One), "De Krans" (The Wreath), "De IJzeren Hein" (Iron Henry), "De Brandweer" (The Fire Department), "De Arabier", "De Zaza", and "De Blauwe Pilaar".

237

After this discussion of the ups and downs of builders, rental agents, and licensees, we shall once more return to the arrangers of the organ books. They too have their vicissitudes, for the same combination of encouraging and disheartening developments seems to afflict them. Of the two men who before the war handled the major part of the music for street organs, Carl Frei and Piet Maas, only the latter remained after the war. Until 1952 he worked for Perlee and after that he continued in business for himself until his death in 1959 of a heart attack at the age of 60. We could not let this opportunity pass without voicing our great and warm appreciation of the numerous achievements of this quiet and hard worker, which remain to bear witness to his abilities. Because before the war everyone's attention was directed towards Carl Frei, and because afterwards his compositions still remained the most beloved ones in the repertoire, Piet Maas never really received the recognition and admiration which he really deserved.

After 1945 the empty space Frei left had to be filled. In the domain of the fair organs, for which he had also arranged much music before the war, this opening was filled by Louis van Deventer at Brummen. Besides Carl Frei, Van Deventer is the only person who combines the qualities of expert organ builder and capable arranger. During the last few years, Marcel van Boxtel, who has also earned fame in the organ world as a photographer of organs, especially fair organs, has also been earning a name for himself doing arrangements for these instruments.

As far as street organs are concerned, since 1947 the author of this book has tried to fill the vacancy somewhat, but the past few years he has limited himself drastically and has mostly arranged patriotic songs and classical music. The popular music for street organs has been done by the young Gerard Razerberg of Middelharnis, whose arrangements elicit general appreciation and admiration. The energy which he has to expend to keep pace with the repertoire of the Dutch organs now borders on the incredible.

About the capacities of the various arrangers and the qualities of their books emotional discussions often take place. I recall that on one occasion an organ man called me over and pointed to a young man listening to the music from the other side of the street. "That boy over there", he said, "took off his coat for you yesterday!" It seemed that he had taken my side when someone criticized a book I had made, and it turned into a fight. From across the street he smiled at me, a wide grin. Should I have treated him to a drink?

We could go on and on, for there are many more incidents worth mentioning . . . dramatic ones, such as the time lightning struck the home of Louis van Deventer and started a fire which destroyed not only all his personal belongings, but also many precious organ parts; or the crash of various organs which have so far not been rebuilt, including "De Kleine Freese", "De Barometer", and above all "De Cementmolen". The last one smashed into a low viaduct at high speed as it was being transported by truck in the summer of 1956. Fortunately there have been many happy events about which we could write much more, such as the triumphant trips abroad of "De Klok", "De Arabier", "De Drie Pruiken", "De Jupiter", "De Turk", and the now wrecked "Barometer", or the many successful street organ meets and contests.

We shall not go into this subject any further, because something much more vital deserves our attention now: namely, the steps which have been taken since 1955 to preserve the fair organs and to find new destinations for those fair and dance instruments which could no longer be used as such and therefore had be snatched from destruction with the utmost dispatch.

The Fair and Concert Organs

Like the pierement, the fair organ was at its peak during the period 1920-1940, the time when the big fairs were also at their zenith. Do you remember the majestic steam carousels, the shimmy palaces, the "Ride-e-o", the "Caterpillar", and the combined attractions such as the "Cocktail Palace", the "Mixture Palace", and the big dance tents? In these establishments were to be found the largest and most beautiful fair organs ever built, among them many of the 89-key Gavioli type. The older of our readers may remember the beautiful Gavioli in the steam carousel of Hubert Wolfs which later went to J. W. Janvier's carousel, or rather, to the "Cake-Walk" connected with it. Tragically, this instrument was completely destroyed in the carousel fire at The Hague in 1946. Another famous 89-key Gavioli was "De Negen Beelden" (The nine statues), which could be admired at the Ride-e-o of the brothers A. & N. Hommerson. It is too bad that this organ was taken to Germany after the war, but at least it was preserved! Of the German instruments to be seen at the fairs, the Ruth-instruments were particularly striking. Most of the big fair organs were repaired and supplied with books by Carl Frei. These books were fastened to each other in batches of 100 meters and put down in cases with rounded bottoms. Because the beginning and end of this continuous book series was also fastened together and thus were endless, the whole thing could be played without interruption or attention as a sort of "perpetuum mobile". It took approximately a half hour for such a case of books to play completely through and start over. Carl Frei has also rebuilt various big fair organs and has enlarged them with extra registers (especially violin registers) as with "De Dubbele Ruth" and "De Grote Gavioli". His chef d'oeuvre, however, was the rebuilding of two enormous 110 key organs, a Marenghi with

240

which A. H. Kunkels booked such big successes in his dance tent, and a Mortier which the brothers Hommerson commissioned him to rebuild and which could be admired in their "Wembley Attraction".

Alas, after the war much had changed at the fairs, too. Most of the big attractions did not return . . . even the steam carousels disappeared. And even for those fairs that did reopen, it became increasingly difficult to keep the organs working. The cost of labor, rent, and maintenance had risen enormously. Because in addition to this, the very atmosphere at the fairs had changed, the outlook for the fair organs was rather dismal.

The "Kring van Draaiorganvrienden" thought the time was ripe for action. Before the leases were given out in 1956 to the fair concessions, a circular was sent to the city councils of all cities where fairs were to be held, asking that preference be given those who had attractions with organs wherever possible. We quote the following passages from this pamphlet "Often the old fair atmosphere is stifled by the raucous and nerve-wracking blaring of loud-speakers that try to out-screech each other and have crowded out the charming and attractive fair organ. Concessions with amplifiers are sometimes willing to pay more for a lease than those who still keep the organs, for the latter have to pay extra costs and expend extra effort in various respects. It is self-evident that it would be a great loss to the Netherlands if these culturally and artistically valuable instruments were to disappear from the scene." Fortunately, in many instances the reaction was favorable and we may now say that since then a change for the better has taken place. Many of the old organs have been kept in service, and in fact in some cases fair people have bought new organs in order to recapture the old fair atmosphere. It would take too long to mention each and every organ which has been saved by name, but a word of homage, respect, and warm appreciation is due the many men who kept their instruments working or started off on the road with organs in spite of difficulties with transportation, space, and maintenance.

However, the movement to preserve those fair organs still in use did not bring a solution to another important phase of the problem: what could be done with those instruments which would never again appear at a fair because they belonged to owners who had in the meantime sold their attractions? It was urgently necessary to find a solution to this problem with the greatest haste, for concerned here were the biggest and most beautiful organs, and these especially were threatened with extinction. It speaks well for the fair personnel involved that in most cases they just could not bring themselves to sell the organs along with the concessions involved to foreign business people. Special praise in this respect is due the brothers A. & N. Hommerson, C. M. Vermolen, A. H. Kunkels, and Reinhard Dirks. However, the pity which these managers felt for the organs would do little good if something were not done speedily. Most of them were stored in old sheds or under lean-tos in open fields and threatened to become irreparable because they were not used or kept up or protected from the ruinous effects of sun, rain, wind, dampness, leaks, worms, etc. . . .

How could these instruments be preserved as part of the musical heritage of the Netherlands? In seeking a solution to this problem, the "Kring van Draaiorgelvrienden" used as a point of departure two basic thoughts which were presented in the form of rhetorical questions in "Het Pierement" of February 1, 1956:

"Do we not live in an age in which government takes over more and more of the responsibility of protecting those cultural objects which, due to changes in the economic and/or social structure can no longer be maintained by private individuals?"

"Is there not an important task for government and those institutions subsidized by government especially in those cases where not only is maintenance of objects of historical importance at stake, but, far more important, the preservation of objects of actual folkloristic value, whereby, incidentally, the musical-romantic desires of a proportionately large but thus far unobtrusive segment of our population, particularly in our large cities, can be satisfied?"

The practical effect of these two basic ideas was elaborated in the following plan, proposed in the same issue of "Het Pierement":

"Either city councils or foundations subsidized by those who work toward the preservation of folklore and/or the recreation of the population in a broad sense could buy the retired organs from their owners with advice from our Circle. Then they could have them completely restored and keep them serviced regularly, as well as adding to the repertoire periodically."

Concerning the use to be made of these former fair organs, we had numerous suggestions, among them concerts in parks or recreation areas in the same spirit as open air concerts by orchestras on a bandstand, concerts on national holidays, concerts in honor of certain important guests such as key government figures from foreign countries or at exhibitions and sports events and in winter, at skating rinks. That was the general outline as it was conceived five years ago, and one city immediately set a good example: Utrecht. Upon our advice the foundation "Stadsontspanning Utrecht" (Utrecht Recreational Board) bought the 89-key organ, "De Lange Gavioli", from the

Hommerson brothers and had it restored by Louis van Deventer. On December 17, 1955 the rejuvenated "Lange Gavioli" was inaugurated as a municipal organ with great festivities and thus became the first of the new, fourth category to originate alongside the street, fair, and dance organs . . . namely, the concert organ. Our gratitude to the foundation "Stadsontspanning te Utrecht" for this pioneer work. We must also note here that this same organization in conjunction with the "Kring van Draaiorgalvrienden" organizes a big national street organ competition every four years, sponsored the exhibition "Van speeldoos tot pierement" (From Music Box to Pierement) in Hieronymus-plantsoen in Utrecht, which drew over 14,000 visitors during the 8 days it was held, and created the foundation "Museum van speeldoos tot pierement" for which the groundwork was done by the exhibition of the same name held in 1956.

At the initiation of "De Lange Gavioli" we wondered whether the 17th of December, 1955 would become a milestone. Will Utrecht's example be followed by other cities? If we were to have to give our opinion of how things have gone during the past five years, again our answer would have to be, disappointing on one hand, encouraging on the other. It is disappointing . . . even sad . . . that not one other city council or government-sponsored institution has followed Utrecht's lead. And this in spite of the fact that we have repeatedly pointed out the urgency of decisive action at almost all the organ contests and meets held in so many places since 1955. Must these venerable instruments then succumb because of a lack of vigorous initiative in our governmental agencies which are stifled by red tape? Or are our authorities afraid of jeopardizing their careers if they should suggest the "far-out" idea to their superiors of buying a concert organ? It is conceiv-

244

able. In any case, where are these superiors? Is it possible they are afraid not to be able to use, maintain, and repair the instruments properly? There is no need for any apprehension, for in practically every city of our country there are voluntary organ enthusiasts who are eager to help. They would enjoy having the privilege! The relationship between the officials and these volunteers need give rise to no fears either. If we may make a suggestion: foundations could be created to operate and maintain local concert organs, and the boards of directors could be made up of representatives of the authorities involved as well as enthusiastic and expert organ friends.

At least some degree of hope may be derived from the fact that during the years 1956-1960 a number . . . unfortunately, not all by far . . . of concert organs were rescued by private parties and institutions. It is unnecessary to dwell upon the great expenditure of time, effort, and especially, money that this represents.

The biggest concert organ saved in this way is the 89-key Gavioli, "De Grote Gavioli", formerly belonging to the fair manager Reinhard Dirks and bought by Mssrs. A. and J. Waerts at Assendelft-Zaandam. After a thorough restoration by Perlee, this organ gave its first public concert on April 30, 1958. It is again mounted in its original fair wagon, although now riding on pneumatic tires, and gives concerts all over the country and has even made a trip to Fontainebleau. It is a poignant commentary on human mortality that in France no one was acquainted with this type of organ any longer. The glorious era of the creator, Ludovic Gavioli II, is that far in the dim past! The amount of work being done in the province of Friesland was tremendous. In Sneek a former fair manager, Mr. R. Kooistra, bought the 78-key Ruth organ, "De Harp", which had served in the autoscooter of C. M. Vermolen. Now it is being cared for as a concert organ by the Sneek organ connoisseur, Klaas Ruardi. Douwe Beintema in Drachten bought the 89-key Gavioli, "De Troubadour" from another fair manager, K. Stuy. Not only fair organs, but also dance instruments unable to find work in their original occupation were transformed into concert organs and bought by private parties. The Frieslanders once again bore the brunt of this undertaking. The Kussendrager brothers of Gorredyk bought the Mortier organ "De Canadees" (The Canadian) and had it restored by Stelleman, who also did another dance instrument, "De Grote Dorus" (Big Dorus), subsequently used as a concert organ. This instrument was bought by P. Carpay of Leeuwarden. It could be considered the "big brother" of "De Zwarte Dorus" (Black Dorus), a Gavioli street organ which had become the property of Mr. Carpay earlier after having been on the fair circuit with Dorus van Es, nicknamed "Zwarte Dorus" because of his black hair.

In any event, we may state with great satisfaction that at least three of the most beautiful prewar fair organs will be preserved as concert organs. The two largest ones were bought from the Hommerson brothers by the foundation "Museum van speeldoos tot pierement". These are the 96-key organ, "Dubbele Ruth" (the biggest organ built by Ruth, deriving its name from the two organ cases built one behind the other) and the 110-key Mortier, "De Schuyt", rebuilt by Carl Frei. This one was christened thus in honor of Mr. J. J. A. M. Schuyt of Singapore, who made possible the purchase of both instruments by offering an interest-free loan. "The Schuyt" was carefully restored in the summer of 1960 by Carl Frei, Jr. With gratitude we announce that this restoration was carried out only because of a generous contribution by Prince Bernhard-fonds.

"De Grote Gavioli" restored in 1958, now the property of the Messrs. Waerts of Assendelft/Zaandam.

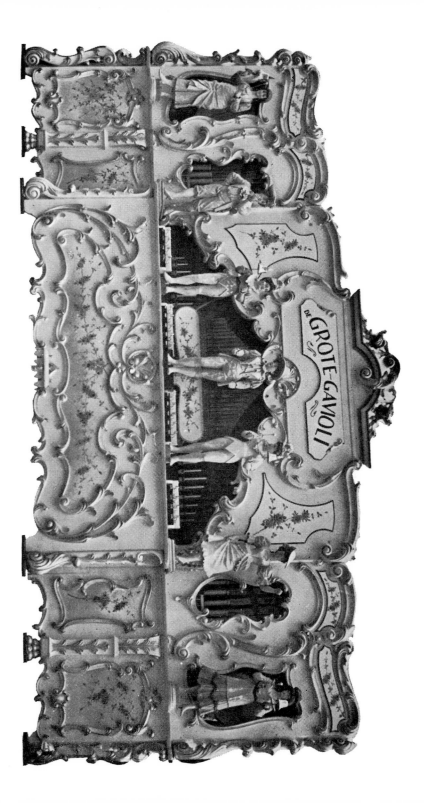

The third of these organs is the 110-key Marenghi rebuilt by Carl Frei and known as "Het Kunkelsorgel" after the owner, Mr. A. H. Kunkels at Maasniel (near Roermond in the southern part of Holland.) He had repeatedly raised cries of distress because he could not find a suitable shelter for the organ and moisture and other enemies of woodwork had already started their deadly work, when a few Haarlem enthusiasts decided to take it under their wing. On January 25, 1958 they moved it to Haarlem and since then it has been sheltered in the workshop of one of the men, Theo van Zutfen. He and other Haarlemmers have had the courage to take on the particularly extensive restoration of this organ, with the assistance of the able expert, Karel Struys. With experience, patience, and perseverence an important job is being done.

Thus it appears that thanks to private organ enthusiasts who have taken the responsibility for the salvation of these instruments upon their own shoulders, November 17, 1955 has become a milestone on a road which will come to an end only when the last instrument that can possibly be saved has been restored and has found its niche as a concert organ.

CONCLUSIONS:

What moral may at this point be drawn from the history of automatically-playing musical instruments "from music box to pierement", or more accurately, "from music barrel to concert-organ", and what conclusions can be derived from the foregoing?

The historically-rooted responsibility of preserving the mechanical musical instruments in whose development Holland has played such a significant role, rests on Holland's shoulders. These instruments may be divided thus:

1. Those instruments which still have a part to play in our society, or can have one again in the future. Apart from automatically playing carillons, which we shall not mention in this section of our book, they all belong to the family of book organs:

the street organs or pierements.

the fair organs insofar as they are still so used.

the old fair and dance organs still in existence which can ,no longer be employed as such and can be preserved only by giving them a new identity as concert organs.

2. Those instruments which have no practical application for the present but even so, must be preserved in view of their historical value . . . in other words, the typical museum pieces.

Is Holland doing its job properly, and will all these instruments be saved? We can state the following on this subject:

The pierement will be preserved if these observations are given the necessary consideration:

The public should give adequately to the organ man who behaves as he should and presents an instrument which plays well. The reward should increase proportionately as the organ satisfies higher musical and aesthetic standards. This should be used as a guiding principle. Attention should be given the pierement and the operator should be treated with respect and in no case with contempt, for he must not only be certain of a reasonable income, but also must be able to enjoy his work. However, if the men are provocative in any way or if the instrument does not meet the standard requirements, then these suggestions do not apply. And now comes an important point. If someone should have a complaint about an organ or its operators, he should state very clearly which instrument or person is involved to whichever authorities he turns. Many of the citizens of our large cities failed to do this in the past, and have consequently provoked general prohibitions by their vagueness, thus hurting innocent organ grinders.

The authorities should take into consideration as much as possible the reasonable desires of the organ operators when issuing permits to them, and if the city ever is divided into sections, the advice of the "Kring van Draaiorgelvrienden" should be sought. In any event, closing any more business streets to organs because of the density of the traffic should only be done where absolutely necessary. The police should investigate complaints very carefully. When there seems to be some truth in it or when there is found to be a transgression, something needs to be done, of course, but only against the guilty man, not against the entire group in the form of general prohibitions and ordinances.

The organ licensees should rent only organs that play well, or if they own an instrument, they should keep it in good condition. They should be have properly and stick to the letter of the law, which in this case is laid out explicitly in the permit. If they don't do this, they ruin things not

---

The Ruth concert organ "De Harp", now the property of Mr. Kooistra of Sneek.

250

only for themselves, but for their colleagues as well. They undermine the position of the organ and the people connected with it and furthermore, make it difficult for the public, the authorities, and the police to keep their part of the bargain.

Our fair organs will survive also if, at the time the permits are issued, some attention is paid the thoughts set down in the circular from the "Kring van Draaiorgel-vrienden", of which we quoted several sections on page 234, and if visitors to fairs give preference to those *with* organs.

Concerning the idea of concert organs, generous financial help from governmental areas, whether town or national, is imperative. This goes for those which have already been restored and are in use as well as the ones which are still awaiting restoration and for which careers as concert organs still have to be found . . . or created. What we have written on this subject in "Het Pierement" of February 1, 1956, still goes (page 242). It would be ideal to have a national restoration fund from which money could be appropriated for use in restorations.

When all these requirements have been met, we shall not have to fear the preservation of the foregoing instruments, for there are sufficient organ builders who will be able to care for the instruments in our country. Notwithstanding, we want to present two suggestions to promote a positive development and to prevent a decrease in the number of valuable organs.

The first is directed at private organ fans. In many smaller cities and towns no professional organ grinders work because there is insufficient space to operate an organ. In order to stimulate interest in the pierement here, a concert organ should be bought if it is at all possible to collect the necessary funds for it, and the cooperation of other enthusiasts is indispensable. On Saturday afternoon, national holidays, and summer evenings, in other words, in your leisure time you can give concerts with this organ. Out of the proceeds you can pay the costs (maintenance, new music, shelter, etc.), while the surplus can be put to good use in the "Museum van speeldoos tot pierement".

The second suggestion is aimed at those in an official capacity. It would be highly advisable to designate the most valuable old organs as public property so that they could not just be dismantled. We would then be immune to the behavior of certain businessmen who in a most degrading manner abuse the financial position of people or institutions who want to save an organ from doom and try to do "business" in a most suspicious manner by threatening, "You pay me fl . . . . (an exorbitant sum) for the organ, or else I'll make kindling wood out of it!"

All instruments that no longer have a practical use should be collected in the national museum "Van speeldoos tot pierement". In this museum the instruments can be preserved and used exactly as they were when they were still providing entertainment in the home or on the street, according to the nature of the device involved, for an instrument is not just put on display. No, a demonstration of the way it functions is given as clearly as possible to the visitors. They can play the instruments themselves, and each one produces music in the style of the era from which it originated. In a sense this is already in effect, although the museum is only provisionally set up and consists for the time being of only one large room. However, with a subsidy from some governmental or other source, it would be possible to realize the plans for a museum set up on a grand scale, which would have the attractive qualities of other museums but offer a refreshing and cheerful contrast to their quiet and stiff immobility because it would vibrate with a richly varied and predominantly romantic liveli-

253

ness. This proposed museum would consist of three departments.

The first would consist of several smaller rooms, each decorated as a salon from a different period. In this intimate atmosphere one could then enjoy the music of music boxes, Floten-Uhren (flute clocks), reed organs, and other salon instruments.

The second would contain one or more large halls to house the cafe piano, the orchestrions, and the dance organs. Special dance evenings could be planned.

The third would have to be set up in the open air, in the form of a little old-fashioned town where early types of street instruments could roam the streets, playing at will. One would encounter the cylinder organs, the street pianos, and the early book organs, played by street musicians from times long gone by. In the windows of the little shops of this town, the documentary material of the museum could be exhibited, and they would also have another function. If a visitor should wish to avoid an encounter with these musicians out of a feeling of embarassment or self-consciousness, he would only have to turn to a shop window with rapt attention and moreover, would be able to look at things which are genuinely interesting. (It would not have to turn out the way it did with a friend of mine who once pretended to be deeply interested in whatever was in a shop window in order to listen undisturbed to the music of a pierement. When suddenly he heard a snicker behind him, he realized that he was staring at a display of ladies' lingerie, in which he had not the slightest interest!) In addition to all this, the open air part of the museum could be set up as a recreation area with as the major attraction, "De Dubbele Ruth", "De Schuyt", and other large concert organs which could take turns giving concerts.

Does all this sound like a dream? Well, we do live in a materialistic age . . . and yet, why could it not come true?

A Brief Discography

A record is to be brought out in the foreseeable future of the most important mechanical musical instruments discussed in this book and to be found in the museum, "Van speeldoos tot pierement" in Utrecht. It will be pressed by C. N. Rood, also under the name "Van speeldoos tot pierement".

The same company has produced records of the playing of the carillon of the Westertoren in Amsterdam by this author, no. HX 1201 (The Glowworm, The Clock Is Playing, Circus Renz, De Postkoets) and no. HX 1194 (national songs).

The most important records of the street organs are: the many recordings of the Groningen street organ "De Arabier", produced by Philips, of which we make special mention of the 33⅓ rpm record "Organ Grinder's Serenade no. 4" (P 08027 L) on which one can listen to the music discussed in this book from the movies "De roverssymfonie" and "Dreigroschen Oper". Besides this there is a 45 rpm record with the two overtures by Rossini "La Gazza Ladra" and "The Barber of Seville" (422 286 PE) and finally, the 33⅓ rpm "Marching with the Arab" (P 08031 L).

Philips (Decca) has issued a 45 rpm record of the street organ "De Gouwe" (The Golden One) with Friesian songs and a 33⅓ (LQ 60409).

Philips (Fontana) has also put out several 45 rpm records of the street organ "De Turk", as well as a 33⅓ rpm of marches and serenades (660515 TR).

Philips has produced a long playing record of the street organ meet held July 10, 1958 in Delft, no. P 13086 R.

From the catalogue of Philips recordings, we finally call your attention to the 45 rpm record "De Speeldoos" (The

Music Box) with 12 melodies of different music boxes from the museum mentioned above (no. 422 282 PE).

Bovema has brought out records of the street organ "De Jupiter".

Three concert organs discussed in the last chapter of this book can also be heard on records, namely "De Grote Gavioli" (amongst others, Mill-rec MEP 1001 and Imperial IPE 5019), "De Harp" (C. N. Rood HX 1187) and "De Schuijt" (C. N. Rood HX 1208).

Of the fair organs which at present are still used as such, a series of records is to brought out under the trade name "Tivoli". The first 45 rpm record in this series (no. 43006) is already commercially available.

This survey does not attempt to be complete. Information on recently-issued organ records can always be found in "Het Pierement", published quarterly by the "Kring van Draaiorgelvrienden", editor J. P. van der Bel, Marktweg 301, Den Haag, The Netherlands.

Fair Organ records are somewhat difficult to obtain in the United States, but readers may obtain several albums by writing to the Vestal Press Record Department, 3533 Stratford Drive, Vestal, New York 13850.

Records of fair organs are also available through the Leslie Brown Bookshop, 95 High Street, Stockton-on-Tees, England, as well as Traction Engine Enterprises, 52 Eden Road, Walthamstow, London E17, England.

261

262

263

SOME OTHER FINE BOOKS FROM THE VESTAL PRESS

PLAYER PIANO TREASURY
by Harvey N. Roehl

The complete scrapbook history of the Player Piano in America, with all its variations — orchestrions, reproducing pianos, band organs, and all the rest. Lavishly illustrated. $10.00

PUT ANOTHER NICKEL IN
by Q. David Bowers

The fascinating story of the coin-operated pianos and orchestrions that once graced the land but now reside mainly in private collections. A large handsome book, with over five hundred large, clear illustrations of these wonderful instruments. $15.00

REBUILDING THE PLAYER PIANO   by Larry Givens

Anyone with a reasonable amount of mechanical ability can bring an old player piano back to life by following the information given in this easy-to-understand book. Tells how players work, what must be done to put them in operating order, and where to obtain the materials to do the job. $6.95

A GUIDEBOOK OF AUTOMATIC MUSICAL INSTRUMENTS
Edited and compiled by Q. David Bowers

This is a valuable reference work with about 600 large pages of important material on automatic music devices of all sorts, with literally thousands of illustrations. Volume I is devoted to the player piano, coin pianos and orchestrions, street and barrel pianos, and reproducing pianos. $5.95, paperbound.

Volume II covers Disc music boxes, cylinder music boxes, band organs, calliopes, player reed organs, and many miscellaneous topics. $5.95, paperbound.

Combination price for Vol I and Vol II together is $10.95, or you may order the deluxe hardbound library edition for $12.95.

The Vestal Press also publishes many service manuals for automatic instruments and catalogs of historical interest. Ask for a free catalog. All prices postpaid.

Order from your favorite bookstore, or directly from

THE VESTAL PRESS
3533 STRATFORD DRIVE
DEPT P
VESTAL, NEW YORK 13850